DEVELOPMENTS
in
BIBLICAL
COUNSELING

DEVELOPMENTS
in
BIBLICAL COUNSELING

J. Cameron Fraser

Reformation Heritage Books
Grand Rapids, Michigan

Developments in Biblical Counseling
© 2015 by J. Cameron Fraser

All rights reserved. No part of this book may be used or reproduced in any manner whatsoever without written permission except in the case of brief quotations embodied in critical articles and reviews. Direct your requests to the publisher at the following address:

Reformation Heritage Books
2965 Leonard St. NE
Grand Rapids, MI 49525
616-977-0889 / Fax 616-285-3246
orders@heritagebooks.org
www.heritagebooks.org

Unless otherwise noted, Scripture taken from the New King James Version®. Copyright © 1982 by Thomas Nelson. Used by permission. All rights reserved.

Printed in the United States of America
15 16 17 18 19 20/10 9 8 7 6 5 4 3 2 1

Library of Congress Control Number: 2015937995

For additional Reformed literature, request a free book list from Reformation Heritage Books at the above regular or e-mail address.

Contents

Foreword vii
Preface xi

Introduction 1
Chapter 1: Some Foundational Views of Nouthetic
          Counseling. 17
Chapter 2: Some Criticisms of Nouthetic Counseling... 43
Chapter 3: Some Developments in Biblical Counseling.. 59
Chapter 4: Biblical and Puritan Counseling 91
Postscript.. 109

Bibliography 117

Foreword

Cameron Fraser and I had a lengthy telephone conversation in the early nineties about a counseling situation that prompted the research eventually resulting in this book. I also wrote regular counseling articles for a magazine he was editing at the time for the PCA churches in Canada. Now, two decades later, he has asked me first to critique the book manuscript and then to write this foreword.

I was blessed in the reading. It is, in my view, fair; apart from merely incidental moments where I offered a few suggested tweaks, I found this to be a valuable and needed book. It would be good to have it in Russian for my ministry abroad—though the readers there would not appreciate the birth pangs and maturing process that many of us in the West have experienced since the inception of the National Association of Nouthetic Counselors and the nouthetic movement. I am excited about this possibility.

Cameron has done excellent work as a reporter. I greatly appreciate where he has landed. God used Tim Keller's article, referenced extensively in chapter 4, to open up to me the world of curing souls—or, "first clean the inside" heart ministry. I believe this graciously and clearly lays bare the extremely important matter of careful case-by-case ministry to the heart, as the best of the best—the Puritans—have done.

I speak as a *practitioner*, commending to you this work of a reporter. Though I still fumble, bumble, and stumble after more than thirty-five years of soul cure (both counseling and training), I do so much less than at the beginning of this long learning curve. I speak as an insider in the sense that my ordained focus for pastoral work has been soul cure. I speak as a *pioneering* practitioner, a voice in the wilderness, attempting to carry the heartbeat of my esteemed mentors—several of whose names appear in these pages—to my home region in Canada and then from Kiev, Ukraine, to the Russian-speaking church. I speak as a *solo* pioneering practitioner, largely working alone, with periodic check-ups. Here I have repeatedly had an uncanny experience. Compelled by Scripture, conscience, and the refinement arising from frontline ministry, I periodically checked back with my mentors, in person and in print. When I did, I consistently found that my wobbling steps landed on the warm asphalt of the trajectory just laid down by our second-generation leaders. So it is from these years of face-to-face soul cure and training of leaders that I speak. I speak as an inside practitioner from a distant pioneering setting.

Christian reader, I envision numerous benefits as you ingest Cameron's reporting contained between these covers. Chapter 3 on the developments in biblical counseling is brief, but distills much valuable research. It references essential works, pointing the reader to sources for further profitable study. This chapter is fair and equitable to differing leaders as their positions and concerns are placed before the reader. It stimulates growth in the sincere Christian reader. Seek application as you read.

First, consider the question, What is your understanding of the distinct work of counseling? Can you articulate the believer's task of counseling activity—a pastoral activity distinct from Christian education, discipleship, encouragement, and help in times of crisis? Numerous first- and second-generation leaders have presented their definitions. I have formulated my own as *soul cure*. What is yours? Does the ministry sphere of helping sufferers find a welcome home in your descriptive definition of counseling?

Second, consider this question: In your work with people, do you spend most of your time where the problem is greatest? We could state it another way: Do you keep the main thing the main thing? The Puritans always addressed the heart, whether they were addressing natural behavior, helping to renew the mind, or weaning affections from things created. For them, what the heart did not do was not done. What about your own work with people?

Third, consider applying the author's concluding statement to your calling within the Shepherd's rescue plan. You will read, "This is surely a positive development in biblical counseling." Ask the question, How am I developing? What is your next step for becoming more competent to counsel others in your place and time? If there were one application from this book that the Spirit of counsel would bring to you, what would that be? I sound the refrain to our national leaders and student groups: "You don't know truth unless you do it." If you wince at something in this book, demonstrate your correction in soul-cure work. If you judge something to be imbalanced, show in ministry what you see as balanced practical theology. Don't rest in theoretical critique; show the good news.

As you prepare to turn the page, know that I place before you a Puritan image. You have lingered with me on the porch. I will not detain you any longer. Step now across the threshold (the author's preface) and then into this well-ordered house. Our guide will take you through three rooms, each highlighting five recurrent themes—and then into a fourth, where parallel themes can be found. Take your time exploring every nook and cranny, pondering how each theme may help in your development. May the Spirit of counsel use the reporting work of our brother Cameron to stir you to grow in wise ministry to souls.

Now, enter in.

—Ron Harris, DMin
Biblical Counselor,
Trainer, and Author

Preface

I grew up in the Scottish Highlands in an environment as theologically conservative as could be found anywhere. The denomination to which I belonged claimed to be Reformed in doctrine, worship, and practice. Yet in one area of practice, little effort was made to be biblical or Reformed. Those with mental illnesses or suffering from depression were routinely referred to a mental hospital, where their treatment followed standard secular psychiatric practice.

In 1975, I began studies at Westminster Theological Seminary in Philadelphia. There, I was introduced for the first time to the concept of biblical counseling being pioneered by Dr. Jay E. Adams. Adams became a full professor of practical theology in that year. He then left the following year to engage in a writing ministry. This was followed by further teaching at Westminster Seminary in California (founded in 1980), and then church planting and pastoral ministry with the Associate Reformed Presbyterian Church. Following his retirement, Adams and others founded the Institute for Nouthetic Studies, now based in Simpsonville, South Carolina.

I never did study counseling directly under Adams, although I took a preaching course from him and sat in on one of his counseling classes. After he left the seminary, his courses were taught by his friend and colleague John Bettler. My future wife, Margaret, enrolled in a two-year program in 1976 with a particular interest in counseling, her first degree having been in psychology. She took a number of courses with Dr. Bettler, who was also of great personal help to us prior to our marriage in 1978.

I did not enter immediately into pastoral ministry; but, shortly after I did, Margaret and I were approached by a couple having marital problems. We counseled them together using a biblically based workbook by Adams's colleague Wayne Mack.[1] The couple was motivated to make changes, and we found that having them follow simple biblical directives really worked.

However, as time went on and we were faced with more difficult cases resulting from abusive backgrounds, we found that there were genuine believers who honestly wanted to obey the Bible, but felt unable to do so because of emotional and psychological dysfunctions. In particular, treating clinical depression as sin only seemed to make things worse. No doubt, a number of factors were in play, including our own inexperience and, yes, sinful thought patterns in those we sought to help. But increasingly we felt out of our depth.

During this time, we were introduced to the writings of Larry Crabb, and I well remember when I first came across (and read aloud) the following passage:

---

1. Wayne A. Mack, *A Homework Manual for Biblical Counseling* (Phillipsburg, N.J.: P&R, 1980).

> I am unalterably opposed to any line of thinking that undermines the concept of personal responsibility, and I find myself in general agreement with those who insist people are accountable for choosing godly responses to life's situations. Nevertheless, I am concerned that our renewed emphasis on responsible choices may tend to promote a superficial view of sin. Sin appears to be defined exclusively in terms of our behavior. What we *do* constitutes the sum total of our sin problem. If how we are behaving is the root problem, then it follows that the solution to difficulties like marital conflict is simple: Find out what you are doing wrong, then choose to do right. Do something different; stop living unbiblically and start living biblically.
>
> It is true that no Christian growth is possible without obedience. To emphasize obedience and to reject psychological thinking that understates the need for obedience is to reflect biblical truth accurately. But to concern ourselves with nothing more than chosen acts of obedience fails to take into account the complexity of human life as revealed in the Bible.[2]

It seemed like a thinly veiled criticism of Adams (and indeed I believe it was). Crabb had written his own *Basic Principles of Biblical Counseling*,[3] which sought to integrate biblical teaching with psychological insights. This was something Adams flatly rejected as unbiblical. But what Crabb wrote seemed to ring more true to real life as we were experiencing it.

---

2. Larry Crabb, *The Marriage Builder: A Blueprint for Couples & Counselors* (Grand Rapids: Zondervan, 1982), 9.

3. Larry Crabb, *Basic Principles of Biblical Counseling* (Grand Rapids: Zondervan, 1975).

Some years later, I sought the counsel of Dr. Adams on a difficult case that, in my view, involved a misuse of one of his books. In our short telephone conversation, which he squeezed in between counseling appointments, he was both helpful and gracious. He insisted that he could speak only in general terms and that I was free to accept or reject his advice based on my familiarity with the actual situation.

I also sought the advice of Drs. J. I. Packer and Paul Stevens at Regent College in Vancouver, near where we lived at the time. Coincidentally, I was beginning a doctor of ministry program through Trinity Evangelical Divinity School based in the Chicago suburb of Deerfield, Illinois. By special arrangement, I was permitted to do part of my work under the supervision of Dr. Packer. A project was conceived comparing the counseling theories of Adams, Crabb, and the Puritan Richard Baxter. (Dr. Packer's 1954 doctoral thesis at Oxford—now available in book form—was "The Redemption and Restoration of Man in the Thought of Richard Baxter: A Study in Puritan Theology.")

In the event, the project became unmanageable (at least for me) and never did reach completion. It was replaced by two separate research papers: one on Adams and the other on a different aspect of Baxter's work. It is the Adams paper that forms the original basis of the present work. It was completed in 2003, and nothing further was done with it until I was asked to write an article for the *Haddington House Journal* (*HHJ*), edited by Dr. Jack Whytock. This appeared in the 2011 *HHJ*.

Dr. Whytock, although based in Prince Edward Island, Canada, spends part of each year teaching in different parts of Africa. He passed the article on to two Bible colleges there. One used it to help teach students and answer some questions that had been raised about the history of Christian counseling. A lecturer at the other college was researching the topic and found the article helpful. Dr. Whytock has also encouraged students generally to read it in order to gain an understanding of the context for this movement.

In the summer of 2013, I mentioned the article to Jay Collier, director of publishing at Reformation Heritage Books (RHB), who invited me to send him a copy. He later told me that RHB was interested in possibly publishing a revised version of the article and two book reviews (originally published in the 2012 *HHJ*) I had submitted for consideration. It was clear that the article would need updating, and this has been done to some extent along with incorporating more (but not all) of the original research paper. Parts of the book reviews have also found their way into the present work.

I am grateful to Dr. Packer for his willingness to supervise my original research paper and for his kind recommendation of the present work; to Dr. Whytock for publishing the article and book reviews and permission to include material from them in this book; to Dr. Richard B. Gaffin Jr. for help with Greek terms; to Karla Grafton, archivist at Montgomery Library, Westminster Seminary (Philadelphia) for her prompt and efficient help in tracking down citations; to my son, James, who likewise helped with his customary patience, checking sources at the T. S. Rendall Library, Prairie Bible College, Three Hills, Alberta; to Lauren Berkhouse, Executive Assistant and Development Assistant, Christian Counseling and Educational Foundation, for prompt and helpful responses to various inquiries; to Jay Collier and Dr. Joel Beeke of RHB for their kind consideration; to RHB staff members for their careful editing; and to Donn R. Arms of the Institute for Nouthetic Studies, who has been most helpful in promptly answering several questions and offering to critique the manuscript. My interaction with his most serious criticisms can be found in the postscript.

Many thanks to Ron Harris for his helpful suggestions as well as for his gracious foreword. Ron has been active in biblical counseling for many years. As part of this, in 1991 he founded Wellspring of Life, a biblical counseling ministry in Canada. He directed it until 2002, when he and his wife, Linda, moved to Ukraine to develop church-based biblical counseling there and in other Russian-speaking countries. Now back in Canada, Ron continues to train and develop counseling resources for leaders at home and abroad through Storehouse of the King. He has authored an eight-book series in Russian, *Resources for Biblical Counseling*. As a professional counselor trained in the nouthetic/biblical tradition, his voice of experience adds authenticity and balance to my role as a sympathetic outsider more comfortable in the role of a reporter.

As always, I wish to express appreciation to my wife for her insightful help and support. Thanks also to Bob Derrick, Ian Crooks, Roderick Gray, and Marc Jagt for their willingness to critique the manuscript and offer suggestions, several of which were implemented. Any remaining infelicities are, of course, my own.

I am not an expert in counseling theory or practice. I have nothing original to offer, other than to pass on helps I have learned from others. My style is more that of journalistic reporting than scholarly analysis, but I am encouraged that others whose opinions I respect have seen some value in what I have written and have suggested that it might be suitable for more public consumption.

Introduction

In his landmark work *Competent to Counsel*, Jay E. Adams challenged the dependence of contemporary Christian counseling on clinical psychology and psychiatry with their secular assumptions.[1] He argued that counseling is fundamentally the work of the Holy Spirit, who uses the Bible, sacraments, prayer, and fellowship with God's people to effect personality and behavioral change. It follows that only Christian believers, and specifically pastors who are equipped to teach God's Word, are "competent to counsel." This book set the stage for what Adams perceived to be a counseling revolution, to which he gave the name "nouthetic counseling," a term which will be more fully explained later.

---

1. The term *counseling* is sometimes used interchangeably with *psychotherapy*, although some would make a distinction between the two. Broadly speaking, on this latter understanding, counseling deals with observable behavior and helping people cope with difficult circumstances, whereas psychotherapy probes deeper into the subconscious motivation that lies behind external behavior. It is assumed that the latter practice requires training in psychotherapy or what is sometimes called *professional* (as distinct from *lay*) counseling. This distinction is not always made and is, in any case, one which Adams would reject.

Competent to Counsel rapidly became a best seller and was translated into several languages. A number of works followed and gave rise to what came to be known as the nouthetic counseling movement. The Christian Counseling and Educational Foundation (CCEF) had already been established in suburban Philadelphia in 1968, two years before the publication of *Competent to Counsel*. This was followed in 1976 by the National Association of Nouthetic Counselors (NANC), with headquarters in Lafayette, Indiana. The former serves as a counseling and training center in association with neighboring Westminster Theological Seminary (where Adams was teaching at the time). The latter was to accredit counselors, counseling centers, and counseling training centers.

David Powlison is currently executive director and a faculty member at CCEF. In his work *The Biblical Counseling Movement: History and Context*, he traces the history of the movement thus begun until almost the close of the twentieth century. He provides some useful background on the influences of Adams's early life leading up to his development of nouthetic counseling. Born on January 30, 1929, into a nonreligious family, Adams was converted as a teenager after a neighborhood friend initiated a street-corner discussion on the truthfulness of the Bible. This led Adams to read the New Testament for himself, and over a period of two months he came to understand and believe the gospel. His conversion was "apparently unmediated by social or emotional inducements; the Word of God had spoken and the human creature had believed. The unadorned biblicism of this conversion established a characteristic theme; the way Adams himself had changed would reappear in the emphases he would bring to the tasks of counseling twenty years later."[2]

Adams began attending a conservative Presbyterian church. Through the pastor's influence, he decided to attend Reformed Episcopal Seminary in Philadelphia. There he came under the influence of Robert Rudolph, the head of the systematic theology department. Rudolph was "noted for his zeal for conservative Protestant orthodoxy, the adversarial atmosphere of his classroom, and his passionate conviction that true believers needed to separate from error rather than engage in cool discussion."[3]

Powlison further develops Adams's personal history, noting particularly the influence of O. Hobart Mowrer, a psychologist who "had begun to challenge Freudian theory, to describe people as morally responsible, and to call troubled and troublesome behavior 'sin.'"[4] Attendance at one of Mowrer's lectures led to Adams interning with him for a six-week period. This "proved to be a dramatic turning point."[5]

Another influence, not fully developed by Powlison, was Cornelius Van Til's presuppositional apologetic method. Van Til's major contribution to apologetics and his influence on the Westminster school of thought was his stress on the need to engage unbelief—and indeed all thought systems—at the level of their fundamental presuppositions. He stressed the biblical antithesis between faith and unbelief and argued that

---

2. David Powlison, *The Biblical Counseling Movement: History and Context* (Greensboro, N.C.: New Growth Press, 2010), 29.

3. Powlison, *Biblical Counseling Movement*, 29.

4. Powlison, *Biblical Counseling Movement*, 35.

5. Powlison, *Biblical Counseling Movement*, 35.

the consistently Christian approach is to reason from the presuppositional basis of Scripture rather than to seek common ground with the unbeliever.

In the introduction to *Competent to Counsel*, a footnote reminds us that Van Til "has demonstrated that at bottom, all non-Christian systems demand autonomy for man, thereby seeking to dethrone God."[6] Thus, in his book *Cornelius Van Til: An Analysis of His Thought*, John Frame can say:

> I believe that the "nouthetic counseling" of Jay Adams, which continues to be developed by the Christian Counseling and Educational Foundation, has a strongly Van Tillian thrust, particularly in its antithetical relation to secular psychology and its determination to uphold Reformed, biblical presuppositions in all counseling theory and practice.[7]

However, as Frame points out, there is another side to Van Til that is often missed by sympathizers and objectors alike. Some of his statements stress the antithesis to such an extent that it would appear that the unbeliever has no knowledge of the truth and therefore has literally no area of agreement with the believer. Nonetheless, other statements stress the limiting effects of common grace on the unbeliever's opposition to truth. Frame discusses five ways in which Van Til describes the relationship of antithesis and common grace, concluding:

---

6. Jay E. Adams, *Competent to Counsel* (Phillipsburg, N.J.: Presbyterian and Reformed, 1970), xxi.

7. See John Frame, *Cornelius Van Til: An Analysis of His Thought* (Phillipsburg, N.J.: P&R, 1995), 394.

> I would suggest that the extreme antithetical formulations with which his thought is most commonly identified and for which he is most commonly criticized do not represent him at his best or at his most typical. Nor do they reflect the full complexity of his thinking on these subjects.... Van Til himself learned much from non-Christians and non-Reformed thinkers, and he taught his students to do the same.[8]

Adams clearly acknowledges the existence of common grace in "restraining sin and allowing people to discover facts about his creation." Also, as we shall see, Adams recognizes "an element of truth" in the secular psychologists he critiques. Nonetheless, his stress is undeniably on the side of antithesis. He believes that it is "nearly blasphemous to claim (as numbers do) that [non-Christian psychological systems], full of errors, falsehoods and anti-Christian teachings, are the product of common grace!"[9]

At the time of his full-time appointment at Westminster Seminary in Philadelphia in 1966, Adams and his family attended a church pastored by John Bettler, who was to be the first pastor to train under Adams. Bettler later became a colleague "second only to Adams in influence upon the nouthetic counseling ministry."[10] There were, however, significant differences between the two men. Powlison notes:

> Bettler's interest in and respect for scholarship and higher education was as habitual as Adams's interest and respect for local church pastors. Bettler worked

---

8. Frame, *Cornelius Van Til*, 210–13.

9. Jay E. Adams, *A Theology of Christian Counseling: More Than Redemption* (Grand Rapids: Zondervan, 1979), 8.

10. Powlison, *Biblical Counseling Movement*, 39.

to open doors for women to train and to counsel; Adams worked to establish a male-dominated model of counseling training and practice. Bettler had been raised fundamentalist and reacted against it, coming to embrace a version of Reformed theology with a broad vision for social and intellectual engagement; he enjoyed the stimulus of dialogue with intellectuals to his "left" who differed from him. Adams reacted strongly against those to his left theologically and ecclesiastically and was comfortable with pastors from separatist traditions.[11]

Adams was by far the more dominant influence in the early days, but Bettler's influence can be seen more clearly in the second generation of biblical counselors.

Powlison observes that the nouthetic counseling movement at the beginning was "a hybrid, combining intellectual and practical features of both the Reformed tradition and the fundamentalist tradition. It hatched within Reformed circles, but found its widest reception in fundamentalist audiences. Adams himself combined Reformed commitments with certain fundamentalist tendencies that made him acceptable to some moderate fundamentalists."[12]

Nouthetic counseling also found a home in, among others, "the milder sorts of charismatics and Assembly of God Pentecostals."[13] The movement spread rapidly throughout the seventies, mainly due to the popularity of *Competent to Counsel*. A major development was the spread of nouthetic principles, initially through the military and then in the

---

11. Powlison, *Biblical Counseling Movement*, 40.
12. Powlison, *Biblical Counseling Movement*, 12.
13. Powlison, *Biblical Counseling Movement*, 12.

National Association of Evangelicals. This was due to the influence of John Broger, one-time director of information for the armed forces. Broger, an evangelical layman of Brethren background, adapted Adams's material into a self-confrontation manual. This was originally self-published and later picked up by Thomas Nelson (1994). In 1974, Broger also founded the Biblical Counseling Foundation (BCF), which emphasizes lay counseling.[14]

The movement stagnated in the eighties as the evangelical psychotherapeutic "counterinsurgency" responded and claimed the position of authority among evangelicals. This included the popular Minirth-Meier clinics, books and radio shows, New Life Treatment Centers (owned by Steve Arterburn), and Rapha (founded by Southern Baptist psychotherapist Robert McGee). Meanwhile, books by theoreticians and practitioners such as Larry Crabb, Gary Collins, David Benner, and Stanton Jones and publications such as the *Journal of Psychology and Christianity* criticized Adams with varying degrees of hostility. The popular pastors' journal *Leadership* eclipsed Adams's *Journal of Pastoral Practice* and sided with the psychotherapists. James Dobson's Focus on the Family organization mushroomed in popularity,[15] and the Recovery Movement—adapting the twelve-step program of Alcoholics Anonymous to every conceivable disorder—found its way into evangelical

---

14. Powlison says 1977, the year Broger retired from government service, but the BFC website has 1974. Broger had also founded the Far East Broadcasting Company following service in World War II.

15. Dobson is no longer with Focus on the Family, having in 2010 founded Family Talk and a new radio broadcast, *Family Talk with Dr. James Dobson*.

churches in a Christianized version. Meanwhile, attendance at the NANC conferences stagnated, and subscriptions to Adams's journal dropped.

In the early nineties another Christian alternative developed. Gary Collins was invited to "remake a tiny, languishing association, the American Association of Christian Counselors (AACC),"[16] and he began publishing *The Christian Counselor* in 1992. By 1995, "the AACC had rocketed past 17,000 members."[17] Meanwhile, however, leading evangelicals like Os Guinness and David Wells were expressing serious reservations about the direction of evangelical psychotherapy. Crabb, in a 1995 *Christianity Today* interview, repudiated the "three-sided model that therapists are qualified to treat psychological problems, pastors spiritual problems, and doctors physical ones." He "called instead for 'shepherding' and 'eldering' relationships in local church communities to replace the 'antiseptic world of a private-practice therapist.'"[18] (It should, however, be pointed out that Crabb, in a subsequent letter to the editor, clarified that he had not intended to debunk the role of Christian psychotherapy. He argued that portraying him as antipsychology badly misrepresented his position, placing him in company where he did not belong.)

---

16. Powlison, *Biblical Counseling Movement*, 204.
17. Powlison, *Biblical Counseling Movement*, 205.
18. Powlison, *Biblical Counseling Movement*, 222. On the next page Powlison notes that, likewise, "Collins's repeated criticisms of psychotherapeutic secularization and professionalization, and corresponding calls for 'biblical' fidelity and church-oriented 'ministry,' gave expression to the new cultural climate within evangelicalism."

Attendance at the NANC conferences began to climb again, and the renamed *Journal of Biblical Counseling* grew from 450 to 2,500 subscriptions between 1992 and 1995. Well-known preacher and author John MacArthur became committed to nouthetic counseling after his Grace Community Church in California was radicalized by a court case. The church was sued for failing to refer to a psychiatrist a young man who committed suicide while being counseled at the church. MacArthur developed a program at The Master's College and Seminary that was organized by Adams's associate Bob Smith and then headed by another associate, Wayne Mack. MacArthur's *Our Sufficiency in Christ* (1991) included an argument for the sufficiency of Scripture in counseling. Trinity Theological Seminary in Newburgh, Indiana, a rapidly growing institution offering programs by extension, hired NANC's former director Howard Eyrich to head up its counseling program. Another significant development has been the Institute of Christian Conciliation, founded by Ken Sande, a lawyer and author of *The Peacemaker* (1991). Overall, nouthetic, or biblical, counseling appears to have experienced a renaissance at the close of the twentieth century.

The turn of the century saw the founding of the Institute for Nouthetic Studies. Later in 2010, the Biblical Counseling Coalition was formed, with Bob Kellemen as executive director and Steve Viars as chairman of the board. Kellemen and Viars teamed up with James MacDonald to edit *Christ-Centered Biblical Counseling*, published in 2013. David Powlison wrote in the foreword that "these pages represent a *development* upon the hard work of a previous generation. You will hear in the core commitments an essential unity with the past."[19] This highly acclaimed book, with twenty-eight chapters contributed by a variety of authors, promises to be a standard work of biblical counseling. A particularly helpful emphasis is on behavioral change that arises out of "the practical implications of the gospel indicatives. We are so prone to move into all the *dos* and *don'ts* of the Christian life that we miss the rich blessings that attend meditation on what God's sufficient Word tells us about our new identity in our Savior."[20]

Besides Powlison's history, the other major critique from within the biblical counseling movement is by Heath Lambert, whose book *The Biblical Counseling Movement after Adams* originated as a doctoral dissertation prepared under Powlison's supervision. It contains a lengthy foreword by Powlison and is dedicated to Adams, "who reawakened generations to the sufficiency of Scripture." Lambert states that his goal is "to honor Dr. Adams by carefully considering his work and the context in which he built it and by highlighting the efforts of men laboring in the tradition he began, to improve on the good work he started."[21] Lambert identifies Powlison as the leader of the "second generation" of biblical counselors.[22]

---

19. David Powlison, foreword to *Christ-Centered Biblical Counseling: Changing Lives with God's Changeless Truth*, by James MacDonald, Bob Kellemen, and Stephen Viars (Eugene, Ore.: Harvest House, 2013), 8.

20. MacDonald, Kellemen, and Viars, *Christ-Centered Biblical Counseling*, 95.

21. Heath Lambert, *The Biblical Counseling Movement after Adams* (Wheaton, Ill.: Crossway, 2012), 47.

22. Lambert, *Biblical Counseling Movement*, 47. Besides Powlison, those Lambert cites as representatives of the "second generation" of biblical counseling include Edward Welch, George M. Schwab, Ted Tripp, Paul David Tripp, and Elyse Fitzpatrick. Wayne Mack (a contemporary of

In the first chapter, Lambert provides personal background on his own interest in counseling as a means of doing ministry well. He then notes the example of the Puritans and those who followed in their tradition. The last work before Adams's *Competent to Counsel* that offered uniquely biblical insights into helping people with their problems was *A Pastor's Sketches*, published in the 1850s by Ichabod Spencer. For more than a century between these two works, Christians "neglected a robustly biblical approach to counseling."[23] Lambert offers nine reasons for this, including the rise of revivalism in the 1800s and the fundamentalist controversy of the early twentieth century. These movements had other priorities than biblical and pastoral counseling. The psychological revolution pioneered by Wilhelm Wundt (the father of experimental psychology) and Sigmund Freud (the father of psychoanalysis) is also mentioned briefly. These and other factors contributed to a theological neglect of the counseling endeavor, which Adams sought to address in *Competent to Counsel* and in the numerous other volumes that followed.

Adams) is a "first generation" nouthetic counselor, several of whose emphases also fit with the "second generation." Lambert gives insufficient recognition (with two references) to John Bettler, cofounder of the CCEF and its director for over thirty years. Bettler was from the start more nuanced about counseling methodology and the value of psychological insights. As Lambert does recognize (*Biblical Counseling Movement*, 104), Bettler sought to be a bridge builder between Adams and his critics in the growing (non-nouthetic) Christian counseling movement, which has generally been more sympathetic to the integration of Scripture and psychology in counseling methodology. Bettler's influence on the "second generation" of biblical counselors should not be overlooked.

23. Lambert, *Biblical Counseling Movement*, 26.

In 2010, Adams wrote a strongly worded blog post in an apparent response to Lambert. He asserted:

> Our self-tagged "second-generation" counselors are nothing of the sort. They are what, more accurately, might be called the third generation or, more precisely stated, the heirs and recipients of an already-refined second generation of biblical counselors that, practically speaking, makes them nothing less than a third.... A great deal of refining, maturing and enlarging of the system has taken place since 1970. Much effort has been expended over the forty-year period, many aspects of counseling have been explored in depth, and a large amount of new material has been mined and made available. What is so surprising—and disappointing—is that this maturing process has been carried on not by our self-styled "second-generationers," from whom we expected so much, but largely by the same small group of "old-timers" who have been a part of the cadre of counselor-theorists who have been "having at it" from (or near) the beginning.[24]

A recurring theme in many of Adams's books is the assertion that he is only beginning to explore the biblical applications to various areas of counseling. He notes that others need to come alongside him to add their writings in areas with which he has not yet adequately dealt. While open and generous to those with differing gifts and emphases within the nouthetic counseling movement, Adams is insistent that,

---

24. Jay Adams, "Second Generation Counselors?—Part 1," *Institute for Nouthetic Studies* (blog) June 16, 2010, http://www.nouthetic.org/blog/?p=3571.

in order to complement his work, they must share his basic commitment to biblical counseling defined as *nouthetic confrontation*. He concludes *Competent to Counsel* with this challenge:

> I am aware of the sweeping implications of the changes I advocate. I am willing to refine my position if I have gone too far. I want to alter any or all of what I have written provided that I can be shown to be wrong *biblically*....
>
> Jesus Christ is at the center of all truly Christian counseling. Although the counseling I have described in this book attempts to recognize and honor him in his rightful place, it certainly contains many defects and inadequacies in doing so. I would welcome enthusiastically the kind of critique which would point out how nouthetic counseling could become more biblical in theory or technique.[25]

Nevertheless, in practice Adams has been resistant to the idea that his basic approach can be improved upon biblically. In the blog post quoted above, he recognizes that times have changed. No longer is medication seen to be nearly the sole solution to life's problems. "Spirituality," including elements of Eastern spirituality, has been added. Everything is now thought to be an "addiction" of one sort or another. He chides the "second generation" of biblical counselors for paying insufficient attention to these developments. Rather, they are too preoccupied with "widening the tent" of biblical counseling and becoming acquainted with their "eclectic" brothers. "They no longer discern the need for believers to assert the sort of

---

25. Adams, *Competent to Counsel*, 269.

antithesis to the world that was once deemed all-important."[26] Elsewhere, Adams asserts that, among the "second generation," there are to be found "a number of the old unbiblical ways that we thought we had put to bed." Among these are an unhealthy emphasis on feelings and a superficial use of Scripture rather than solid exegesis.[27]

A fairly persistent criticism of Adams is that his "approach to counseling is more a reflection of [his] personality than anything else. He tends to be a somewhat confrontational guy, and he's a confrontational counselor."[28] Although Adams strongly disagrees,[29] others argue that there is evidence to suggest that the personalities of counselors and counselees and the relationship established between them are integral to the counseling process.[30] The extent to which individual counselors' personalities influence their understanding of counseling theory, including the application of Scripture, may be more of a factor than Adams acknowledges. Nevertheless, as he points out, in critiquing the views of those from whom we differ, "it is not the persons, as persons, whom we must challenge."[31] Thus, in what follows, I have tried to avoid dealing with the

---

26. Adams, "Second Generation Counselors."

27. Jay Adams, "For Now…," *Institute for Nouthetic Studies* (blog), October 1, 2010, http://www.nouthetic.org/blog/?p=3845.

28. Gary Collins, "Door Interview: Dr. Gary Collins," *The Wittenburg Door* 47 (February–March 1979): 13. Quoted in Powlison, *Biblical Counseling Movement*, 186.

29. Jay E. Adams, *The Christian Counselor's Manual: The Practice of Nouthetic Counseling* (Grand Rapids: Zondervan, 1973), 18–20.

30. John D. Carter and Bruce Narramore, *The Integration of Psychology and Theology: An Introduction* (Grand Rapids: Zondervan, 1979), 113–14.

31. Adams, *Theology of Christian Counseling*, 7.

personalities of Adams, his colleagues, and his critics, focusing instead on their teachings.

This study will attempt to outline some basic themes of nouthetic counseling as originally developed by Adams and on which he continues to insist. Then we will note some criticisms from "outside" before reporting on developments from "within." A final chapter will observe how some of these developments have a certain affinity with Puritan approaches to counseling that Adams rejects, but which may in fact point in a more consistently biblical direction.

Chapter 1

Some Foundational Views of Nouthetic Counseling

This chapter will outline Adams's development of a biblical approach to counseling defined as *nouthetic*. It will do so under five headings, each of which will also appear in the next two chapters, with a slight wording change for one of them in chapter 3.

The Sufficiency of Scripture

A central biblical passage in Adams's overall approach is 2 Timothy 3:14–17. An entire book, *How to Help People Change*,[1] is devoted to this text, and it occurs frequently in Adams's other writings. *The Christian Counselor's Manual* notes that the passage outlines four steps, which "set forth plainly the four basic activities involved in biblical counseling." There is a judging activity based on biblical standards; a convicting activity by the ministry of the Holy Spirit (John 16:8); a changing activity; and a structuring activity, providing the godly discipline necessary for effective change and growth.[2] In

---

1. Jay E. Adams, *How to Help People Change: The Four-Step Biblical Process* (Grand Rapids: Zondervan, 1986).

2. Adams, *Christian Counselor's Manual*, 95–97.

A Theology of Christian Counseling, Adams says, "According to this passage the Word was designed to transform behavior." This transformation has two phases: an instantaneous one in which a sinner is regenerated and justified, and a gradual one in which the process of sanctification takes place.[3]

Nouthetic counseling implies that an unbeliever cannot be counseled in the proper sense of the term because counseling by definition involves the process of sanctification. Thus, unbelievers must be evangelized first. Only if and when they respond positively to the gospel can they be counseled according to biblical principles on the assumption that the sanctifying work of the Holy Spirit has begun.[4]

Adams takes 1 Corinthians 10:13 as a proof for the sufficiency of Scripture for counseling:

> If no Christian faces unique tests in life, and if Paul can say to the church at Corinth (living in an entirely different age and culture) that what happened to the Israelites is pertinent also to them (cf. vss. 6, 11), a counselor may be assured that he will face no truly unique problems in counseling. There are just so many basic common themes of sin and no more.[5]

The biblical counseling so described contrasts with "the counsel of the ungodly" as found in Psalm 1:

---

3. Adams, *Theology of Christian Counseling*, 36.

4. Jay E. Adams, *Essays on Counseling* (Nutley, N.J.: Presbyterian and Reformed; repr., Grand Rapids: Zondervan, 1972 [originally *The Big Umbrella and Other Essays on Christian Counseling*]), 97–112.

5. Adams, *Christian Counselor's Manual*, 22.

Both the counsel and those who give it are ungodly. It is ungodly (1) because it competes with and tries to overthrow God's counsel, (2) because it is inspired by Satan and (3) because (intentionally or otherwise) it is given by those who rebelliously side with the devil. Over against such counsel (and in direct opposition to it) the psalm places God's Word (vs. 2).[6]

The Definition of Biblical Counseling

Adams uses the term *nouthetic* to define biblical counseling. Based on the Greek *noutheteō* and its cognates (see Acts 20:31; Rom. 15:14; Col. 1:28; and 3:16), nouthetic counseling consists of at least three basic elements.[7]

First, the term is frequently used in conjunction with *didaskō* (to teach). But whereas *didaskō* simply suggests the communication of information, *noutheteō* presupposes the need for change:

The idea of something wrong, some sin, some obstruction, some problem, some difficulty, some need that has to be acknowledged and dealt with, is central. In short,

---

6. Adams, *Theology of Christian Counseling*, 4.

7. In *Competent to Counsel*, Adams writes, "The words *nouthesis* and *noutheteo* [sic] are the noun and verb forms from which the term 'nouthetic' comes" (p. 40). For "a good discussion of the term," a footnote on page 44 references an article by Behm in Gerhard Kittel, *Theological Dictionary of the New Testament* (Grand Rapids: Eerdmans, 1967), 4:1019–22. However, neither Kittel nor any of the standard Greek lexicons use the word *nouthesis* at all. They refer to the verb *noutheteō* and the nouns *nouthesia* and *nouthetēsis*. I am indebted to Marc Jagt for pointing this out. In *The Christian Counselor's Manual*, Adams identifies the New Testament word for counseling as *nouthesia* (17), and in *A Theology of Christian Counseling*, he calls it "the principal and fullest biblical word for counseling" (ix).

nouthetic confrontation arises out of a condition in the counselee that God wants changed. The fundamental purpose of nouthetic confrontation is to *effect personality and behavioral change*.[8]

The second element in nouthetic counseling is that problems are solved by verbal means. Adams quotes Trench as saying, "It is training by word—by the word of encouragement, when this is sufficient, but also by that of remonstrance, of reproof, of blame, where these may be required; as set over against the training by act and by discipline which is *paideia*.... The distinctive feature of *nouthesia* is the training by word of mouth."[9]

Adams says the third element "has in view the purpose or motive behind nouthetic activity. The thought is always that the verbal correction is intended to benefit the counselee. This beneficent motive never seems to be lost, and is often quite prominent."[10]

These three elements came to be classified as "*change* through *confrontation* out of *concern*,"[11] now popularly known as the three Cs. Adams rejects the idea that "confrontation" has a negative implication. "Nothing could be further from my mind as I use it," he says. The word implies authority but not belligerence. It might have been as well to speak of "nouthetic consultation" except that it would be too "neutral."

---

8. Adams, *Competent to Counsel*, 45.

9. Adams, *Competent to Counsel*, 45. Cf. R. C. Trench, *Synonyms of the New Testament* (Grand Rapids: Eerdmans, 1948), 112–14.

10. Adams, *Competent to Counsel*, 49.

11. Jay E. Adams, *Ready to Restore: The Layman's Guide to Christian Counseling* (Phillipsburg, N.J.: Presbyterian and Reformed, 1981), 9.

Adams writes, "The positive aggressiveness and willingness to put one's self on the line in reaching out to help another in a face-to-face encounter that is inherent in *nouthesia* is better expressed by the word confrontation. For me it is a good and *more* positive term than consultation."[12]

Adams cites Paul's relationship with the Ephesian elders in Acts 20 as an example of "nouthetic pastoring." The goal of this type of pastoring and counseling is "love from a pure heart, and a good conscience, and a sincere faith" (1 Tim. 1:5).[13] It is biblically based and thus holds out hope for real change as the Holy Spirit applies His Word to concrete human dilemmas.

Relationship to Psychology and Psychiatry

Adams claims that he is open to the insights of psychology to the extent that they support and "fill out" the basic commitment of nouthetic counseling. He frequently expresses frustration at the perception that he is antipsychology.[14]

Adams's relationship to psychology and psychiatry is clarified in his inaugural address as professor of practical theology at Westminster Seminary in 1975. In his address titled "Counseling and the Sovereignty of God," Adams asserts two thoughts: (1) God is sovereign and His Word applies to all of life and (2) God in His Word assigns to pastors the task of shepherding His sheep. Because of these two truths, the work

---

12. Jay E. Adams, *What about Nouthetic Counseling?* (Grand Rapids: Baker, 1976), 33.

13. Adams, *Competent to Counsel*, 42–54.

14. Adams, *What about Nouthetic Counseling?*, 31.

of counseling necessarily falls to those (pastors) whom God in His sovereignty has so ordained. It is their task to help people learn to love God and their neighbors. Since all personal and interpersonal difficulties involve a violation of these two great commandments (of love for God and neighbor), it is the pastor's responsibility to help people relate to others and God Himself. However, when the counselor attempts to do this, he finds other persons (psychologists and psychiatrists) competing with him. Therefore, Adams contends, "it is not the pastor who is responsible for the overlap; it is the psychologist on the one side, who has moved his fence over on to the pastor's territory, and the psychiatrist on the other, who has also encroached upon his property. Unfortunately, until recently, pastors have been all too willing to allow others to cut their grass."[15]

Does this mean that there is no legitimate role for the psychologist and psychiatrist? Adams replies: "No, you misunderstand me. It is exactly not that. Remember, I said clearly that they live next door to the pastor. My problem with them is that they refuse to stay on their own property. I have been trying to get the pastor to mow his lawn to the very borders of his plot."[16]

After discussing the role and value of experimental psychology, Adams turns his attention to psychiatry, noting:

> In the United States psychiatrists are physicians, who (for the most part) use their medical training to do little else than prescribe pills.... The pastor recognizes the effects of Adam's sin upon the body; he, therefore, has

---

15. Adams, *What about Nouthetic Counseling?*, 18.
16. Adams, *What about Nouthetic Counseling?*, 18.

no problem working side-by-side with a physician who treats the counselee's body as he counsels him about its proper use. From the days of Paul and Luke, pastors have found kinship with medical personnel. Why, then, does the psychiatrist present a problem? Certainly it is not because of his medical background. The problem is that he will not stay in his own backyard. He keeps setting up his lawn chairs and moving his picnic table onto the pastor's property.[17]

In *How to Help People Change*, Adams states that there is "no necessary relationship between psychology and Christian counseling." The "integration" of the two is the new "in" word. Nevertheless, he adds:

> It would be valuable for Christians in experimental psychology, and in other areas of psychology, who also view counseling as an illegitimate activity of psychologists, to unite with Christian counselors in exploring the areas where, occasionally, the two touch (1) to discover in what ways the two activities complement one another and (2) to develop ways and means for dialogue and cross-fertilization. Integration of this sort is not only possible but desirable.[18]

Although Adams refers to various psychologists and schools of psychology throughout his writings, he principally criticizes three of the best-known and most influential theorists: Freud, Rogers, and Skinner. He describes Freud and Skinner in their different approaches as being united in believing that

---

17. Adams, *What about Nouthetic Counseling?*, 19.
18. Adams, *How to Help People Change*, 39–40.

counseling "can only be done from the point of view of expert knowledge.... Only the experts know how. They alone possess the proper knowledge, methods and techniques.... They are held in awe by laymen in a fundamentally gnostic pattern."[19] Rogers, on the other hand, adopted a "common knowledge" approach "based upon the idea that all men have adequate knowledge and resources to handle their problems.... The therapist...shares time with a client in order to help him to help himself."[20]

Adams adds Mowrer as a representative of the "common knowledge" approach. He sees things differently from Rogers.

> Instead of failure to live up to one's potential as the root difficulty, he thinks man's problems stem from bad behavior.... Mowrer uses words like religion, sin, and guilt, but he drains them of biblical meaning and then fills them with humanistic content....
>
> But because he has no Savior, Mowrer is like the priest that stands daily ministering the same sacrifice that can never take away sin.... Consequently counselees can never be satisfied and have peace about sin."[21]

Adams, writing in 1973, observed that Mowrer was departing from past practice by developing "Integrity Groups" as a means for counselees to confront and encourage one another.

Adams contrasts these different approaches with what he calls the "divine knowledge" approach. Here he introduces his biblically based model, noting:

---

19. Adams, *Christian Counselor's Manual*, 73–74.
20. Adams, *Christian Counselor's Manual*, 84.
21. Adams, *Christian Counselor's Manual*, 86–87. The fact that Mowrer committed suicide in 1982 tragically reinforced Adams's point.

Some Foundational Views of Nouthetic Counseling 25

> The resources are not in the outside expert, the resources are not in the counselee, nor are they in ourselves; the resources are in God....
>
> It is time that we all put our hearts and minds and abilities to the problem of exegeting the Scriptures, not merely academically, but pastorally. We also need to look hard at the world out there *in the light of the Bible* to discover how *biblically* these two fit together. We must know men's problems and we must find God's answers.[22]

Adams acknowledges that there is "usually an element of truth reflected by every false position."[23] Yet the truth is distorted so that the distortion only dimly approximates the truth itself:

> The element of truth reflected in Freudianism is that people *do* exert significant influence upon one another. Obviously parents influence children, church authorities influence members, etc....
>
> There is an element of truth also poorly reflected by Skinnerianism. The environment is of great influence upon man. It is true that making changes in the environment may be useful in counseling. Reward and punishment are biblical concepts; the Bible is replete with exhortations and laws that depend upon the reward/punishment dynamic. However, to say this is a far cry from accepting Skinnerian presuppositions or methods....
>
> There is an element of truth reflected by what Rogers does...in his reaction to the expert who considers man not responsible for his behavior. Rogers wants a

---

22. Adams, *Christian Counselor's Manual*, 97.
23. Adams, *Christian Counselor's Manual*, 76.

responsible man; yet he has failed to postulate a responsible man by declaring man independent of God....

There is some reflection of the truth in Mowrer, dimly perceived. God made us social creatures; we need one another.... When we come together it should be for mutual edification.... But self-atoning Integrity Groups can never be that; true society exists only among the redeemed community of God—the Church of Jesus Christ.[24]

Thus, while Adams has little if any sympathy for psychiatry as currently practiced, he does see experimental psychology as a useful source of scientific research, while rejecting the humanistic approach of most clinical psychology. At the same time, he recognizes "an element of truth" even in those with whom he most disagrees. However, Adams is highly critical of those who seek to integrate humanistic psychology with Scripture. He believes that the "study of psychology in depth coupled with a smattering of scriptural data can lead only to the grossest misstatements regarding man and the solutions to his problems." More strongly yet, Adams states:

In my opinion, advocating, allowing and practicing psychiatric and psychoanalytical dogma within the church is

---

24. Adams, *Christian Counselor's Manual*, 76–88. Adams makes further criticisms of group therapy, including the suggestion that such groups encourage blame-shifting and slander by having members air their feelings about people not present, contrary to the reconciliation/discipline dynamic of Matthew 18:15–17. Of course, he then states, not all groups are wrong. The family, church, and youth groups, for instance, can be powerful influences for good, but there are clearly defined biblical limits for groups, and Christians must learn to be guided by these limits.

every bit as pagan and heretical (and therefore perilous) as propagating the teachings of some of the more bizarre cults. The only vital difference is that the cults are less dangerous because their errors are more identifiable, since they are controverted by existing creedal statements.[25]

Although Adams acknowledges "an element of truth" in Freud, Skinner, and Rogers, that element is quite small. While he finds the same small element of truth in Mowrer as in the others, Adams elsewhere acknowledges Mowrer's considerable influence on him. He even expresses gratitude to God for Mowrer's role in helping Christians understand that the mentally ill can be helped. This is because of Mowrer's emphasis on personal responsibility, which nevertheless needs to be reinterpreted biblically. Because Adams's bent is toward stressing responsibility and avoiding blame shifting, it is understandable that he would see more redeemable value in Mowrer than in someone like Freud. So much is this the case that a consistent criticism of Adams has been that he fails to acknowledge just how much he has been influenced by Mowrer.[26]

According to Adams, labeling that is not biblical "is false and, therefore, harmful. To call a man psychotic, neurotic, psychoneurotic, etc., is dangerous and should be avoided."[27] He says:

> The Scriptures plainly speak of both organically based problems as well as those problems that stem from sinful attitudes and behavior; but where, in all God's Word,

---

25. Adams, *Theology of Christian Counseling*, xi–xii.
26. Powlison, *Biblical Counseling Movement*, 185.
27. Adams, *Christian Counselor's Manual*, 43n5.

is there so much as a trace of any third source of problems which might approximate the modern concept of "mental illness"? Clearly the burden of proof lies with those who loudly affirm the existence of mental illness or disease but fail to demonstrate biblically that it exists. Until such a demonstration is forthcoming, the only safe course is to declare with all of Scripture that the genesis of such human problems is twofold, not threefold....

Apart from organically generated difficulties, the "mentally ill" are really *people with unsolved personal problems*.[28]

Adams does acknowledge:

There is a possibility that some of the bizarre behavior which one meets in so-called schizophrenic persons, stems from organic roots. For example, Osmond and Hoffer have proposed a theory based on the idea that perception is distorted in some persons by a chemical misfunction....

According to the Osmond-Hoffer theory, the root of the problem does not lie in the person's mind or emotions, nor does the problem arise from sinful behavior, but involves faulty perception (i.e. chemically distorted perception).[29]

If this theory is correct, Adams says, there is conclusive evidence that "mental illness" will have to be reclassified as "perceptual illness." However, the term *schizophrenia* itself is similar to the words "red nose." One may have the latter for

---

28. Adams, *Competent to Counsel*, 29.
29. Adams, *Competent to Counsel*, 37–38.

any number of reasons, like "boozing, growing a pimple on it, being punched in [sic] it, or getting sunburned. *Schizophrenia*, like the words, red nose, is a non-specific term that says nothing of *causes* but speaks only of *effects* (bizarre or strongly unpleasant behavior). Its use, particularly as the designation for so-called mental *illness*, ought to be discontinued."[30]

What does Adams do with bizarre behavior? Such behavior, he argues, can be caused by at least three known organic possibilities: bodily (glandular) malfunction, drug abuse, or sleeplessness. Faced with bizarre behavior, the counselor should remember that "nothing is wrong with his [the counselee's] mind; he is *not* mentally ill. The problem is with the data that is fed to the mind by the senses. The brain operates properly but on the basis of incorrect data."[31]

It is the counselor's task to point out to the counselee that his life must be lived according to God's Word. Man's body is the temple of the Holy Spirit. Unless he is constantly mindful of this, the counselee will develop sinful patterns and bizarre behavior. In the counseling process, the counselor must therefore "break through the camouflage or the sinful life pattern or attitude that has been developed…in order to help the counselee solve his problems in a biblical manner."[32]

Means and Methods of Behavioral Change

An early chapter in *The Christian Counselor's Manual* establishes that the Holy Spirit is the "Principal Person" in the

---

30. Adams, *Christian Counselor's Manual*, 385n3.
31. Adams, *Christian Counselor's Manual*, 385.
32. Adams, *Christian Counselor's Manual*, 388.

counseling procedure. As such, He is not only to be distinguished from unclean spirits but also identified as the source of all holiness. The fruit of the Spirit is the result of His work. "Christians may not counsel apart from the Holy Spirit and His Word without grievously sinning against Him and the counselee."[33] Counselors may take it for granted that any quality of life or attitude mandated in Scripture is possible and may be acquired through Christ by the work of His Spirit. While "not all *gifts* of the Spirit may be acquired by all Christians…all of the items in Galatians 5 that are said to be His *fruit* are available to every Christian."[34]

The way in which the Spirit effects biblical change is through the patterns of "dehabituation" and "rehabituation." Not just behavioral changes, but a change in the "manner of life" (Eph. 4:22) is called for. Change is a twofold process. It involves both putting off the old manner of life and putting on the new. Thus, it is not sufficient to stop telling lies; one must become a "truth teller" (v. 25). It is not enough to stop stealing; the thief must instead become a hard-working person who shares with others (v. 28). The works of the flesh must be replaced by the fruit of the Spirit (Gal. 5:16–26). The way of the ungodly must give way to the fruit of righteousness (Ps. 1). The disciple of Christ must die to self by taking up his cross (putting off) and following Jesus (putting on). The Christian life begins by turning "*from* idols/*to* the living and

---

33. Adams, *Christian Counselor's Manual*, 6–7.
34. Adams, *Christian Counselor's Manual*, 172.

true God (1 Thessalonians 1:9)." It continues as the believer habitually turns "*from* sin/*to* righteousness."[35]

How does this happen? It is by the "practice of godliness," which leads to "the life of godliness." "If you *practice* what God tells you to do, the obedient life will become a part of you."[36] Habit is a part of life, whether it is learning how to drive or putting toothpaste on a brush. But habits can be evil, as when our hearts are "trained in covetous practices" (2 Peter 2:14). Thus, since God made us with the capacity for living according to habits, counselors must help counselees develop godly habits and lifestyles.[37]

All this talk of human effort must not be misunderstood. We are talking about "grace-motivated effort," not the work of the flesh. It is not effort apart from the Holy Spirit that produces godliness. Rather, it is through the power of the Holy Spirit alone that one can endure. By his own effort, a man may persist in learning to skate, but he will not persist in the pursuit of godliness. "A Christian does *good works* because the Spirit first works in him."[38]

Whereas Satan prompts feeling-oriented living, the Holy Spirit prompts obedience toward God. How, then, is the counselee to be motivated to choose commandment-oriented living over feeling-oriented living? First, he must choose to become in practice what he already is in principle. He must consider himself to be "dead indeed to sin, but alive to God in

---

35. Adams, *Christian Counselor's Manual*, 176–79.
36. Adams, *Christian Counselor's Manual*, 181.
37. Adams, *Christian Counselor's Manual*, 180–82.
38. Adams, *Christian Counselor's Manual*, 186.

Christ Jesus our Lord" (Rom. 6:11). This involves the painful task of crucifying the flesh, taking it to the cross. It is hard, as Paul's struggle in Romans 7:14–25 testifies, but victory is possible through Christ (v. 25). Then there is the motivation of reward and punishment. God Himself motivates by rewards (1 Cor. 3:8, 14; Eph. 6:2; Heb. 11:6). This, together with instructions from Proverbs on such matters as the beneficial use of the "rod" in discipline, should alert us to this biblical principle. Note how the apostle Peter adds further motivations: "Therefore submit yourselves...for the Lord's sake...because of conscience toward God...for righteousness' sake" (1 Peter 2:13, 19; 3:14). The choice of motivation used in any given case depends on the circumstances and individuals involved, with the provision that it is biblical and oriented toward others rather than self.

Although Adams clearly teaches that biblically defined change arises out of a repentant heart, his *emphasis* is on the resulting change in behavior. This is illustrated in a number of ways. Those suffering from problems of fear, anger, anxiety, and depression must come to terms with the relevant biblical directives and act on them. Husbands who find themselves incapable of loving their wives as Christ loved the church, or even as their neighbors, must learn to love them as their enemies. (This, of course, is a tongue-in-cheek statement and a highly effective way of saying that there is no escaping the biblical imperative to love.) Those divorced on unbiblical grounds, that is, other than adultery or desertion by an unbelieving spouse, must repent and seek reconciliation following the "reconciliation/discipline" dynamic of Matthew 18:15–18. If need be, this can lead to the excommunication of the unrepentant spouse, and even of the church of which he or she is a member! This is followed by the declaration that he or she is now an unbeliever and has abandoned the spouse, who is now free to remarry. Ex-homosexuals who have difficulty engaging in sexual relations with their spouses must realize that sexual relations within marriage are a duty. When they give themselves to their spouses in this way, their own sexual difficulties can be overcome.[39]

Adams briefly discusses the fact that believers will persevere to the extent that they abide in Christ (see John 15:5–6). Also, as we have seen, one of the motivations for change is coming to terms with who we are in Christ. The believer must see himself as God sees him—freed from the slavery of sin and raised to newness of life in Christ. Indeed, Adams might argue that his whole methodology arises out of the implications of union with Christ. But when he talks about stressing "the whole relationship to Christ,"[40] he focuses almost entirely on the behavior that arises out of this relationship rather than on the relationship itself and the corresponding motivation that arises not out of duty but out of devotion and love.

---

39. See Adams, *Christian Counselor's Manual*, 348–67, 375–83, 391–425. Cf. Jay E Adams, *What Do You Do When Fear Overcomes You?* (Nutley, N.J.: Presbyterian and Reformed, 1975); Jay E. Adams, *What Do You Do When Anger Gets the Upper Hand?* (Nutley, N.J.: Presbyterian and Reformed, 1975); Jay E. Adams, *What Do You Do When You Become Depressed?* (Nutley, N.J.: Presbyterian and Reformed, 1975); Jay E. Adams, *What to Do about Worry?* (Phillipsburg, N.J.: Presbyterian and Reformed, 1980); and Jay E. Adams, *Marriage, Divorce and Remarriage in the Bible* (Grand Rapids: Zondervan, 1980).

40. Adams, *Christian Counselor's Manual*, 204.

Sin, Suffering, and Satan

In extended exegesis of James 5:14, Adams argues:

> [If] the cause is otherwise unknown (and perhaps even in the case of some known causes) James directed that when the patient discusses his sickness with the elders and prayer is made, the possibility of sickness as a result of sin ought to be discussed. If sin is found in the background of the problem, it must be confessed.[41]

In discussing the use of oil in the James passage, Adams argues that it was for medical use. Therefore, "instead of teaching faith healing apart from the use of medicine, the passage teaches just the opposite." But James did not consider the use of medicine and prayer alone to be effective in the case of patients with unconfessed sin. In such cases, prayer must include confession of sin. "Sin is at the root of some illnesses and may at least be a contributing factor to some complications of other illness." Confession must be made not only to God but also to one another.[42]

Adams is careful to assert that "the Scriptures never represent all sickness as the result of immediate sin or even sinful patterns of life."[43] The examples of Job and of the man born blind (John 9:1–3) are cited as evidence. Yet the Bible teaches that the existence of all sickness goes back to the sin of Adam. It also does recognize an immediate relationship between sin and sickness in many instances. For example, in John 5:14, Jesus says to one man whom He healed, "See, you have been

---

41. Adams, *Competent to Counsel*, 106.
42. Adams, *Competent to Counsel*, 108.
43. Adams, *Competent to Counsel*, 108.

made well. Sin no more, lest a worse thing come upon you." First Corinthians 11:30 states that many of the church at Corinth were weak or sick and some had even died because of abuse of the Lord's Table. Adams concludes, "It would seem that as a regular practice pastors should inquire into the possibility of sin as the root of the sickness."[44] He also points to Scriptures such as Psalms 32:3–4; 38:3, 9; and 51:3, 8 where sin-induced guilt produces psychosomatic symptoms and where confession of sin brings relief and happiness. The psalmist's experience of joy over forgiveness is then shared with others (Pss. 32:8–9; 51:13). Nouthetic counselors, according to Adams, adhere closely to Proverbs 28:13, "He who covers his sins will not prosper, but whoever confesses and forsakes them will have mercy." They also believe that "Depressed persons whose symptoms fail to show any sign of a biochemical root should be counseled on the assumption that they are depressed by guilt."[45]

Despite the disclaimer noted above, one is tempted to wonder how a nouthetic counselor would have dealt with Job without the prior knowledge afforded by the opening chapters of the narrative and without any evidence of organic problems. Adams has been faced with this question before. In *What about Nouthetic Counseling?*, he answers several of the most commonly asked questions, including how his approach differs from that of Job's friends. Adams's answer is threefold. First, "Job's comforters failed to gather data." They came with preconceived ideas into which they tried to fit the situation

---

44. Adams, *Theology of Christian Counseling*, 109.
45. Adams, *Competent to Counsel*, 126.

without first seeking to gather all the information they could. This contrasts with the approach of nouthetic counselors. Second, "Job's comforters failed to believe him in love." Contrary to 1 Corinthians 13:7 ("love believes all things"), they failed to believe Job when he denied their accusation that sin was at the bottom of his troubles. Third, "Job's counselors failed to focus on the real issue." As in many counseling situations, Job's calamity came "through no fault of his own." His problem was "one that nouthetic counselors continually deal with—how to handle suffering for which one is not personally responsible. At first Job handled it really well, but at length it was at this very point that he broke.... It was about this failure that God, the perfect Counselor, confronted Job in the end."[46]

Although Adams states that nouthetic counselors frequently counsel people who are not responsible for their troubles, this point does not come across as an emphasis in his overall approach. This is why questions such as the one about Job are frequently asked. In *The Christian Counselor's Manual*, Adams raises the issue of childhood abuse and its effects. He recognizes that sometimes physical and emotional abuse that combine organic and psychological factors may result in lasting organic damage. But he also wants to stress that "God does hold children responsible for sin from the very first day of their lives." Like David, they are "conceived and born in sin" (Ps. 51:5). The wicked "are estranged from the womb" and "go astray as soon as they are born" (Ps. 58:3). The fact that God does not consider children morally

---

46. Adams, *What about Nouthetic Counseling?*, 49–50.

neutral means that they may be held responsible for "making whatever righteous responses that it is possible for a child to make at any given age. As unredeemed sinners, children will fail to respond as they should. For this they are accountable." As they mature in age, they become proportionately more responsible:

> As capacities enlarge, not only is the capacity for obedience greater, but the capacity for sinful responses is enlarged as well. At any given point in life, therefore, a child is held responsible for doing whatever he ought to be able to do at that age....
>
> While the Scriptures everywhere acknowledge the important place of habit and faithfully describe the hard struggle to put off old sinful ways, they also ring with the assurance that by the Word and Spirit radical changes are possible at any point in life and regardless of what one's background may have been like. There is hope for change in the gospel of Jesus Christ. Therefore, when a child becomes a Christian, he must be taught that much of what he has learned previously must be changed. The former sinful manner of life developed by others and by himself must be replaced by godly ways of living.[47]

"But," Adams asks, "what of the child who has been berated time and again by his parents who has been told in a hundred ways that he is worthless; who is constantly criticized and condemned?" The principle still "remains the same":

---

47. Adams, *Christian Counselor's Manual*, 139–40.

> If he believes what he is told, then that is what he is—a weak person dependent upon others for self-evaluation.... That is why the greatest sympathy and the strongest help that a counselor...can give to a child is to focus not upon what others have done or are doing to him...but upon what God expects him to do in response. Therein lies the hope that at once will honor God and (as a by-product) change his self-concept.[48]

What about the role of Satan in human suffering? Besides Job, there are other biblical examples of this, such as the woman who had been crippled by an evil spirit. Jesus said that it was Satan who had kept her bound for these eighteen years (Luke 13:10–17). This woman's suffering was primarily physical, but Jesus' ministry of exorcism included those such as the tormented man among the tombs who, after the demons had been cast out of him, was found "sitting and clothed and in his right mind" (Mark 5:1–20).

Adams argues that because Satan was bound by Christ's victory on the cross, demonic activity is largely curtailed in the New Testament era. He writes, "This accounts for the rare incidence, if not the entire absence, of demonic possession in modern times. It is possible, of course, that demonic activity is still in the process of being curtailed *as the gospel penetrates* new and previously untouched communities of the world."[49]

---

48. Adams, *Christian Counselor's Manual*, 149.
49. Adams, *Essays on Counseling*, 118.

Adams further holds that "there is no biblical reason to think that demonic possession (or oppression) can occur in the life of a Christian." The simultaneous presence of the indwelling Holy Spirit and an unclean spirit is impossible (see Mark 3:20–30). Adams notes that "more and more frequently failure in counseling has been attributed to the fact of demon possession." He argues that in the light of biblical-theological eschatology "it would seem that a heavy burden of proof belongs to the one who retreats to demon possession as the cause of bizarre behavior. Counselors, in this present era, have every reason to expect that the cause of the problems with which they deal in counseling will be other than demonic possessions."[50]

Adams suggests that current evangelical preoccupation with demonic activity parallels popular interest in the occult. He notes that "Christian counselees, of the sort who before would have become concerned about the assurance of their salvation or about having committed the unpardonable sin, now theorize about having been possessed or oppressed by a demon." He believes that "demon possession or oppression affords a ready-made cop-out from personal responsibility."[51]

The fact that Adams minimizes direct demonic activity today to the point of discounting it does not mean that he downplays the role of Satan altogether. He states, rather, that "Christian counselors should not need to be reminded that they have been called to labor in opposition to the world, the

---

50. Adams, *Essays on Counseling*, 120.

51. Adams, *Christian Counselor's Manual*, 129.

flesh, and the devil. Their task involves not merely a struggle with flesh and blood (that side of the problem is large enough), but also a fight against the supernatural forces of darkness (Ephesians 6:12)."[52] But when Adams goes on to discuss the role of Satan, it is in terms of his strategy, so vividly illustrated in the temptation of Adam and Eve, of having them opt for "the satisfaction of desire rather than for obedience to the commandment of God."[53]

The heart of Adams's treatment of Satan's role, and indeed a central element in his thinking about biblical counseling, is that "it is a clever 'wile' of Satan to tempt men to think that they cannot *do* what God requires because they do not *feel* like doing it, or that they must *do* what they feel like doing and cannot help themselves."[54] Some counselors wrongly encourage counselees to follow their feelings rather than to obey the Word of God. This "is to side with Satan, to solidify the original problem, and to elicit the complications that come from further sinful behavior."[55]

This is not to say that feelings are unimportant. Nouthetic counselors do not *focus* on feelings because they know that "when they focus upon attitudes and actions the proper feelings will follow."[56] To live according to feelings rather than the commandments is therefore not only sinful, it is "to side with Satan." Thus, the influence of Satan is seen, not in

---

52. Adams, *Christian Counselor's Manual*, 117.
53. Adams, *Christian Counselor's Manual*, 118.
54. Adams, *Christian Counselor's Manual*, 118.
55. Adams, *Christian Counselor's Manual*, 121.
56. Adams, *Christian Counselor's Manual*, 136.

manifestations of oppression or possession, but in one's manner of life.[57]

---

57. Powlison notes that Adams "often reiterated a slogan from William Glasser's Reality Therapy—'Act right, feel right.'" *The Biblical Counseling Movement*, 102.

John Frame takes exception to the priority of the intellect over feelings in Adams (as well as in much of Western theology), noting that

> the intellect and emotion are simply two aspects of human nature that together are fallen and together are regenerated and sanctified. Nothing in Scripture suggests that either is superior to the other.
>
> Greek philosophy traditionally presented a different picture: the human problem is a sort of derangement of the faculties. Whereas the reason ought to be in control, unfortunately the emotions often rule....
>
> But the Fall was not essentially a derangement of the faculties within man. It was a rebellion of the whole person—intellect as much as emotions, perception and will—against God. My problem is not something within me; it is me....
>
> Therefore (though my good friend and colleague Jay Adams balks at the suggestion), it is not entirely wrong to substitute "I feel" for "I believe." Of course, when people say "I feel x is the case," they often seek to avoid responsibility for discerning objective truth. That is Adams' point and one that is quite true. But one may use the language of feelings without intending to flee responsibility. Having a belief is, indeed, having a certain kind of feeling *about a proposition*. And when that feeling leads us rightly, that belief, that feeling, constitutes knowledge. *The Doctrine of the Knowledge of God* (Phillipsburg, N.J.: Presbyterian and Reformed, 1987), 336–38.

Chapter 2

Some Criticisms of Nouthetic Counseling

We now turn to some criticisms of nouthetic counseling as developed by Adams, using the same five headings as in the previous chapter.

The Sufficiency of Scripture

We have seen that nouthetic counseling's most basic claim is that the Scriptures provide a sufficient basis for counseling. This claim has been controversial, even among critics most closely identified with Adams's overall theological position.

For instance, a critique from the Continental branch of Reformed orthodoxy comes in the form of J. S. Hielema's 1975 doctoral dissertation, published in the Netherlands. Hielema compares Adams with his Princeton contemporary Seward Hiltner. Regarding Adams, Hielema notes the influence of Cornelius Van Til as well as biblical theologian Geerhardus Vos. Adams's dependence on covenant theology, particularly in his treatment of the family and of Christian education, is also stressed.[1] Beyond this, however, Hielema

---

1. J. S. Hielema, *Pastoral or Christian Counseling: A Confrontation with American Pastoral Theology, in Particular Seward Hiltner and Jay E. Adams* (Utrecht: Elinkwijk, 1975), 158–59.

questions Adams's claim that "it is those views commonly held by Reformed theologians...that I have assumed throughout."[2]

Hielema was writing before the publication of *A Theology of Christian Counseling*, which covers the major *loci* of Reformed theology as applied to counseling. However, I suspect Hielema would still want to ask, "Does an emphasis on 'scriptural counseling...that is wholly scriptural' really appreciate the nature and character of Reformed theology?"[3]

Hielema wonders if a counseling approach stressing that the Bible and the Bible only can be the counselor's textbook does not move in the direction of "the theology of Anabaptism" and "biblicism."[4] Does Adams, he asks, adequately appreciate the ramifications of the "multiform wisdom" of Scripture—a phrase used by John Murray? This implies (quoting Frame) "that a study of nature and the human situation may be necessary in order to determine the proper application of a Scriptural command."[5] Does nouthetic counseling "use all the results of the sciences in its interpretation of the Christian Life—these results interpreted, of course, in the light of Scripture"? According to Hielema, "In Adams' plea to use the Bible as a textbook for counseling we find a serious misunderstanding of the Holy Spirit's work in both the history of Christianity (*corpus christiani*) and the life of the believer."[6]

---

2. Hielema, *Pastoral or Christian Counseling*, 223. Cf. Adams, *Christian Counselor's Manual*, 34.

3. Hielema, *Pastoral or Christian Counseling*, 224.

4. Hielema, *Pastoral or Christian Counseling*, 225.

5. Hielema, *Pastoral or Christian Counseling*, 223. In fairness to Adams, some of his writings suggest that he does, but the criticism persists.

6. Hielema, *Pastoral or Christian Counseling*, 223–34.

Crabb is another critic who discusses the view that the Bible directly answers every legitimate question about life and is therefore a sufficient guide for counseling. Crabb makes the point that one who takes this position must necessarily limit the questions he asks to ones specifically answered in the Bible: "The effect of this viewpoint is to disregard important questions by calling them illegitimate." This is because "*it is possible to give the literal meaning of the text a comprehensive relevance that it simply does not have.*"[7] The result "will often be a nonthinking and simplistic understanding of life and its problems that fails to drive us to increased dependency in the Lord."[8] Crabb argues for another way of viewing the sufficiency of Scripture. It is a framework for thinking through every important question about people, drawing out the implications of biblical data and always remaining within the boundaries that Scripture imposes.[9]

Several critics make a related point that has to do with Adams's perceived minimizing of general revelation in relation to special revelation (Scripture). This objection comes in various forms, but one is most telling: "Adams fail[s] to replicate

---

7. Larry Crabb, *Understanding People: Deep Longings for Relationship* (Grand Rapids: Zondervan, 1987), 55. Crabb offers three illustrations to make his point: a man with strong urges to dress like a woman; a woman who panics at the mere thought of sexual activity with her "loving, patient and considerate husband"; and an anorexic teenager. Powlison takes issue with this, arguing that the Bible does speak to such issues as anorexia: "Larry Crabb and Biblical Counseling," in David Powlison, *Theology and Secular Psychology: Resource Articles* (Glenside, Pa.: Westminster Campus Bookstore, 1992), 7.

8. Crabb, *Understanding People*, 58.

9. Crabb, *Understanding People*, 57–58.

the Bible's own attitude. For example, many of the Solomonic proverbs [evidence] a wide-ranging curiosity about the natural world not dependent on divine revelation: 'much of the wisdom contained in Proverbs could have been discovered by a secular sage of the Ancient Near East or of contemporary America.'"[10]

Powlison quotes the British psychiatrist Roger Hurding who argues that "in his writings as well as in personal conversation, Jay Adams acknowledges the existence of divine common grace.... [But his] seeming neglect of the biblical dimensions of general revelation and common grace *as a developed argument* is, I believe, the main root of at least some of his more disputed opinions."[11] Thus, when Dr. James Hurley of Reformed Theological Seminary was invited in 1993 to evaluate the practical theology department at Westminster in California, "three-quarters of his review involved detailed criticism of the counseling program's commitment" to Adams's model and "to its neglect of the 'common grace' wisdom of the psychologies."[12]

The Definition of Biblical Counseling

Regarding the narrower question of how to define biblical counseling, John D. Carter questions Adams's choice of *noutheteō* as a biblical term. Carter points out that *noutheteō*

---

10. Powlison, *Biblical Counseling Movement*, 171 (quoting John H. Coe, "Educating the Church for Wisdom's Sake or Why Biblical Counseling Is Unbiblical" [Evangelical Society paper, unpublished, 1991], 30).

11. Roger Hurding, *The Tree of Healing* (Grand Rapids: Zondervan, 1985), 285. Quoted in Powlison, *Biblical Counseling Movement*, 172.

12. Powlison, *Biblical Counseling Movement*, 212.

and its cognates occur only thirteen times in the New Testament. He suggests that

> *parakaleo* and its cognate *paraklesis* [sic] make a much more adequate model of counseling from a biblical perspective. These words and concepts are much more central biblically. Together they are translated in the King James Version 29 times as "comfort," 27 times as "exhort," 14 times as "consolation" and 43 times as "beseech" and infrequently as "desire, entreat, and pray." Furthermore and perhaps of greater import, *paraklesis* is listed as a gift to the church (Romans 12:8).... The concept is broad enough to support a variety of therapeutic techniques from crisis intervention to depth therapy and it is a gift given to the church which is clearly different than the gift of prophet or teacher. On the other hand, *nouthesia* represents a rather narrow range of functioning which Christians are to engage in, but does not have the status of a gift to the church and does not have the centrality that Adams wants to give it.[13]

Defining biblical counseling by means of word studies is difficult. This is because different words, each meaning different things, are all capable of being translated *counsel* or *counselor*. For instance, the Hebrew word *yōētz* is used in Isaiah 9:6 and is understood to refer to Jesus as the Wonderful Counselor. It has the Old Testament idea of someone who gives advice, usually to a king. Sometimes the king himself is spoken of as a counselor (Mic. 4:9). The Greek equivalent of *yōētz* is neither *nouthesia* nor *paraklēsis*. It is *boulē*, which has more to

---

13. John D. Carter, "Adams' Theory of Nouthetic Counseling," *Journal of Psychology and Theology* 3, no. 3 (1975): 152–53.

do with carrying out God's will as revealed in the gospel (Acts 20:27; Eph. 1:11). That said, the use of *paraklēsis* does appear to have rich implications to identify what has become known as biblical counseling.

Although Adams makes only limited use of *paraklēsis*, he does refer to it. For instance, he notes, "The guiding and teaching function of the biblical counselor is seen clearly in John 14:26; 16:13. His methods as Counselor are described in John 16:7–15. The Spirit as Counselor is so concerned with counseling by teaching and leading into *truth* that He is specifically designated 'the Spirit of truth' (John 14:17)."[14]

In an interesting footnote, Adams suggests that the gospel of John portrays Jesus particularly as the "Counselor" and is built around the titles attributed to Christ in Isaiah 9:6. He expresses the hope that nouthetic counselors would "undertake the important biblical study of Jesus Christ as Counselor. He was Counselor to men in general and Counselor to his disciples in an even more intimate way."[15]

Elsewhere, Adams has acknowledged that he would prefer to use the words *biblical* or *Christian* to describe his counseling method. He uses *nouthetic* reluctantly because *nouthesia* appears almost exclusively in Paul and is not universal throughout Scripture. Other terms are used by other biblical writers.[16] However, Adams is insistent that the elements of nouthetic counseling as defined earlier encompass the content of true biblical counseling. Several of his critics,

---

14. Adams, *Christian Counselor's Manual*, 5n4.

15. Adams, *Christian Counselor's Manual*, 5n3.

16. Adams, *What about Nouthetic Counseling?*, 1.

on the other hand, suggest that nouthetic counseling is part of the biblical approach but needs supplementing. David Carlson, for instance, proposes a threefold model of counseling styles corresponding to different biblical approaches: "prophetic-confrontational, pastoral-conversational, and priestly-confessional." Carlson places Adams exclusively in the first category.[17] As we shall see, some of Adams's colleagues have also seen the need to fill out the rest of the biblical picture.

Relationship to Psychology and Psychiatry

In his critique of nouthetic counseling, Carter notes that Adams's degrees are in theology and speech, not psychology. He also points out that Adams had experienced only a summer internship with Mowrer, a psychologist known for his research on behavior therapy and his emphasis on taking personal responsibility.[18] This is related to two areas of criticism: that Adams has inadequate training in psychology and that he reflects the influence of Mowrer. Regarding the latter, Carter contends that nouthetic counseling "has all the assets and liabilities of a confrontational-behavioral-responsibility approach (e.g. Mowrer)." The focus is on observable external change rather than internal processes. Adams's "strong emphasis on behavior and confrontation appears to have

---

17. David E. Carlson, "Jesus' Style of Relating: The Search for a Biblical View of Counseling," *Journal of Psychology and Theology* 4, no. 3 (1976): 181–92.

18. Carter, "Adams' Theory of Nouthetic Counseling," 149. Adams also studied with a Freudian psychiatrist at Temple University in Philadelphia, resulting in his book *The Power of Error: Demonstrated in an Actual Counseling Case* (Grand Rapids: Baker, 1978).

come directly from Mowrer and to have blinded Adams to the Scriptures' emphasis on the inner aspects of man in sin." Adams's claim that his approach produces greater and more rapid success is difficult to substantiate, but "one of the reasons for his apparent success is its surface character."[19]

Adams's perceived inadequacies in psychology, according to Carter, are evident in that he "fails to understand the psychologists he most severely criticized, namely Rogers and Freud." His "psychological naïveté" is evidenced by his attributing the concept of transference to "Rogerians and other Freudians."[20] Neither Freud nor Rogers would recognize themselves in Adams's critique. The reason for this "appears to be that he has never read the original authors (or at least understood them) as indicated by his failure to cite their original works." Carter, unless he has overlooked anything, finds only two references to Freud's works and five to Rogers's in Adams's three major works under consideration.[21] Apart from those, Freud and Freudians and Rogers and Rogerian therapy "are repeatedly described from secondary sources." Mowrer and Skinner "are both less frequently and less harshly criticized," although they are also rejected as unbiblical.[22]

Several other critics have implied that Adams lacks psychological training and expertise. Powlison references several and observes that (according to the critics) Adams's alleged

---

19. Carter, "Adams' Theory of Nouthetic Counseling," 153.

20. Carter, "Adams' Theory of Nouthetic Counseling," 154. Cf. Adams, *Christian Counselor's Manual*, 101.

21. Adams, *Competent to Counsel, Essays on Christian Counseling,* and *Christian Counselor's Manual*.

22. Carter, "Adams' Theory of Nouthetic Counseling," 154.

"ignorance and unfairness" relative to the major theorists "arose from an identifiable source. He was indebted to Mowrer far more profoundly than he acknowledged." Adams might "disclaim Mowrer's influence as nothing more than clearing the ground of Freudian influences." Yet, "to critics who read Mowrer and Adams side-by-side, it was evident that the entire structure of [Adams's] theory was Mowrerian."[23] Adams has repeatedly and vehemently denied being a disciple of Mowrer. Yet some critics see this as evidence that he is in fact a crypto-disciple. He "brings secular principles through the back door."[24]

Some have also accused Adams of popularizing the views of psychiatrist Thomas Szasz, author of *The Myth of Mental Illness* and other works (although Adams does not make frequent reference to these works). The late Dr. D. Martyn Lloyd-Jones, in the context of appreciation for Richard Baxter's thirty-five-point distinction between mental and spiritual depression, says: "I do hope that people who tend to follow Thomas Szasz and his popularizer Jay Adams will take all that to heart."[25] The Dutch pastoral theologian C. Trimp is also of the opinion that Adams has replaced Szasz's "social model" with a "religious model" and that this leads to oversimplification.[26]

---

23. Powlison, *Biblical Counseling Movement*, 185.

24. Collins, "Door Interview: Dr. Gary Collins," 13, as quoted in Powlison, *Biblical Counseling Movement*, 185.

25. D. Martyn Lloyd-Jones, *Healing and the Scriptures* (Nashville, Tenn.: Oliver-Nelson Books, 1988), 158. Cf. Richard Baxter, *A Christian Directory*, in *The Practical Works of Richard Baxter* (repr., Ligonier, Pa.: Soli Deo Gloria, 1990), 1:261–67.

26. Hielema, *Pastoral or Christian Counseling*, 244.

Even Adams's closest associates have echoed some of these criticisms. Bettler, Adams's friend and cofounder of nouthetic counseling, is most notable. He believes "many biblical counselors have been unfair to their enemies, the psychologists." He thinks that Adams has "often treated psychologists unfairly, setting up straw men easy to demolish."[27]

Means and Methods of Behavioral Change

In *Dynamics of Spiritual Life*, Richard Lovelace suggests, "The counseling approach which is most likely to help in congregational renewal is a tuned and adapted form of nouthetic counseling."[28] He goes on, however, to make some serious criticisms of the nouthetic approach. He alleges:

> Such counseling simply operates with the Pelagian model of the Christian life common in modern Evangelicalism, assuming that sin problems are only habit patterns of disobedience which can be broken down by the application of will power in a process of dehabituation. This is a view of sanctification which will work in some instances, especially on persons who have been looking for easy victories through faith and neglecting the vigorous engagement of the will. But it does not penetrate the depth of the problem of indwelling sin and provide a dynamic to overcome it. Thus, at times it will amputate the surface manifestations of sin without disturbing the roots of the flesh and produce a pharisaical self-righteousness. In other cases it can lead almost

---

27. Powlison, *Biblical Counseling Movement*, 213.
28. Richard F. Lovelace, *Dynamics of Spiritual Life: An Evangelical Theology of Renewal* (Downers Grove, Ill.: InterVarsity, 1979), 218.

> to despair as the counselee attacks an iceberg of concealed sin with efforts at discipline and will power. This approach to counseling…is not sufficiently evangelical because it fails to see that progress must be grounded in the appropriation by faith of the benefits of the union with Christ.[29]

The charge of Pelagianism—surely the ultimate insult to a Reformed theologian—seems extreme. *A Theology of Christian Counseling*, not to mention Adams's other writings, places him well within the orthodox Reformed understanding of the doctrine of man. Indeed, his chapter on the nature of man is among the most satisfying descriptions of human nature (including concepts of body, soul, mind, etc.) available in print. However, Lovelace's perception is that nouthetic confrontation, by stressing change at the behavioral level, has the appearance of being Pelagian in its inadequate attention to the motives of the heart. Others have made the same charge. Carter goes so far as to say that Adams has two theologies: one (Reformed) which he professes; the other (Pelagian) which he practices in his counseling model.[30]

William T. Kirwan, formerly of Covenant Theological Seminary, offers similar criticisms of Adams's behavioristic use of Scripture:

> Jay Adams advises depressed people to change their sinful behavior patterns: "Go ahead and do it.… *No matter how you feel*. Ask God to help you." That advice takes too mild a view of the fall and its effects on human

---

29. Lovelace, *Dynamics of Spiritual Life*, 220–21.
30. Powlison, *Biblical Counseling Movement*, 174.

functioning. The will, along with the cognitive and affective aspects of the heart, has been badly damaged; to a large extent human beings no longer have control over themselves.[31]

In support of the above, Kirwan quotes Van Til as saying that "before the fall man's will controlled his subconscious life, while after the fall man's subconscious life controlled his will."[32] Adams might well counter that Van Til was referring to unregenerate man without the Holy Spirit's power. Nevertheless, the fact remains that the consensus is widely held that Adams fails to account adequately for the prevailing effects of sin on the will and that his "biblical behaviorism" is theologically deficient.

Hielema's critique supplies a helpful corrective to Adams's emphasis on external behavior over internal processes of the heart. Hielema refers to H. Jonker's term *orthognosie* (or *orthognosis*):

> [Jonker] used this term to elaborate upon the thought that we are not only to be concerned about "ortho-doxy," the right doctrine, but also "ortho-praxis," the right

---

31. William T. Kirwan, *Biblical Concepts for Christian Counseling: A Case for Integrating Psychology and Theology* (Grand Rapids: Baker, 1984), 91. For Kirwan's quote from Adams, see Adams, *Christian Counselor's Manual*, 379.

32. What Van Til says in context is that "the fall of man wrought no metaphysical change in man. We do not mean, therefore, by saying that before the fall man's will controlled his subconscious life, while after the fall man's subconscious life controlled his will, that any real change has taken place in man's metaphysical and psychological makeup. What is meant is that a moral turnover has taken place." Cornelius Van Til, *Christian Theistic Ethics* (Nutley, N.J.: Presbyterian and Reformed, 1971), 49.

deed. The jump from "doctrine" to "deed," Jonker holds, cannot be made. The missing link between "orthodoxy" and "ortho-praxis" is "ortho-gnosis." Ortho-gnosis is the right knowledge of God, the inner attitude of faith. This is indeed a very useful term that should be employed in pastoral theology. If we expect too much from "methods" and "techniques" in the praxis of pastoral work we reduce the Gospel of Jesus Christ to a mere "object." This would prove to be a fruitless and "legalistic" procedure.[33]

Hielema's overall critique, it should be pointed out, is not entirely negative. Among other positive evaluations of Adams throughout his work, he includes a useful and largely favorable comparison of Adams with Calvin on Scripture, discipline, and holiness.[34] This places Adams well within the Reformed tradition in terms of Scripture and its application. But what the quotation from Jonker shows is that Hielema agrees with the widespread consensus that Adams moves too quickly from the biblical text to behavioral application. He does not pay sufficient attention to the cultivation of "the inner attitude of faith." Hielema also quotes Trimp who says it is nothing but "legalistic-methodistic" to view biblical change, as Adams does, to be effected by a "pattern" that is reversed by "beginning an upward cycle of righteousness resulting in further righteousness."[35]

---

33. Hielema, *Pastoral or Christian Counseling*, 263.
34. Hielema, *Pastoral or Christian Counseling*, 170–71.
35. Hielema, *Pastoral or Christian Counseling*, 244.

Sin, Sickness, and Satan

Turning to another area of criticism, Lloyd-Jones was one who considered Adams to be less than fully biblical, especially in his denial of demonic influences today. Lloyd-Jones argued that the view that demon possession was restricted to the apostolic era is "not only dangerous, but…completely unscriptural." This is because "there is no scriptural evidence for saying that the manifestation of demon activity—the activity of evil spirits—ended at that time." He found that demonic activity was "a very, very common cause of people's coming to see the minister, and also to a lesser extent, to some of you [doctors] in general practice."[36] Prior to entering the ministry, Lloyd-Jones was a physician and assistant to Lord Horder, the queen's personal physician. Later, he gained the reputation of being perhaps the greatest English-speaking expository preacher of the twentieth century. He maintained a lifelong interest in medicine, and the above quotation is taken from a talk he gave to physicians on the body, mind, and spirit.

Adams sees current interest in demonology as an unhealthy preoccupation influenced by New Age ideas. In contrast, Lloyd-Jones asserted that demonic activity is on the rise and traced it to "the lowered spirituality and godlessness" of the times. "As godlessness increases and the whole concept of God in the public mind diminishes, you would expect a corresponding increase in manifestations of evil forces."[37] Experimenting with drugs and the occult are mentioned as direct causes, as is indiscriminately seeking after spiritual experiences.

---

36. Lloyd-Jones, *Healing and the Scriptures*, 159.
37. Lloyd-Jones, *Healing and the Scriptures*, 160.

Lloyd-Jones divided the contemporary phenomena into demonic "oppression" and "possession" (a distinction Adams rejects as a misunderstanding of Acts 10:38.) He gave examples from pastoral experience (including symptoms) of dealing with both phenomena.[38] In cases of demonic possession, which are often the result of dabbling with spiritualism or the occult in some form, Lloyd-Jones recommended traditional exorcism. He proposed a different method for cases of demonic oppression that usually involve Christians who have been called to specific ministries and who come under attack by the devil in the form of extreme discouragement and depression. He advised, "You will always be able to deliver them by reasoning with them out of the Scriptures. I do not mean by just quoting Scripture but deploying the whole basic arguments of Scripture concerning salvation, calling and service."[39] Lloyd-Jones's approach is in marked contrast to that of Adams, who asserts that "it would seem vital to effective biblical counseling to presuppose that a counselee is free from such direct demonic influence in this era."[40]

---

38. Lloyd-Jones, *Healing and the Scriptures*, 161–67.
39. Lloyd-Jones, *Healing and the Scriptures*, 168.
40. Adams, *Essays on Counseling*, 120–21.

Chapter 3

Some Developments in Biblical Counseling

The previous chapter outlined some criticisms of Adams and nouthetic counseling from outside the movement. This one will show how some from within the movement developed biblical counseling in a way that ultimately led to the dropping of the term *nouthetic*.

The Sufficiency of Scripture

In *The Biblical Counseling Movement after Adams*, Heath Lambert devotes a chapter to analyzing Eric Johnson's critique of biblical counseling in *Foundations for Soul Care: A Christian Psychology Proposal*. Johnson makes a distinction between "traditional biblical counseling (TBC)" and "progressive biblical counseling (PBC)." He suggests that TBC is committed to the exclusive sufficiency of Scripture in counseling. But the PBC movement has "a more nuanced perspective on the issue, allowing other sources of information to contribute to the Bible's teaching."[1] Lambert critiques Johnson's distinction

---

1. Lambert, *Biblical Counseling Movement*, 125. Cf. Eric Johnson, *Foundations for Soul Care: A Christian Psychology Proposal* (Downers Grove, Ill.: InterVarsity, 2007).

with extensive quotations from both groups, showing that "though some believe that there has been disagreement among counselors concerning Scripture's sufficiency, in truth this is one of the main areas in which there has been no change in the last twenty years."[2]

Those who insist on a biblical counseling methodology begin with the Scriptures. This is their basis. Their writings are filled with biblical exposition, and psychological insights are brought in only in a secondary and tentative manner. In contrast, Christian psychologists often tend to start with psychology and use Scripture to back up their views. Thus, it does not come down so much to whether or not one is committed to the final authority of Scripture in principle. Rather, it is how well and consistently one actually uses the Scriptures in counseling theory and practice. This is how Powlison ends an article titled "Which Presuppositions? Secular Psychology and the Categories of Biblical Thought." He asks three questions:

1. Does the momentum behind a particular idea come from Scripture or psychology?

2. Is the God-ward referent in immediate evidence when discussing human behavior, motives, norms, problems, solutions and so forth? Or is psychology the moving force in a system and Scripture is employed essentially to window dress and prooftext?

3. Do the observations of psychology illustrate and apply biblical categories of thought about human life? Or is Scripture used to provide illustrations,

---

2. Lambert, *Biblical Counseling Movement*, 137. Lambert said this in 2012.

applications and parallels to secular categories of thought?[3]

In the chapter "Frequently Asked Questions about Biblical Counseling" in *Introduction to Biblical Counseling*, edited by John MacArthur and Wayne Mack, Powlison describes the difference between biblical counselors and Christian psychotherapists:

> Most Christian psychologists view the Bible as an inspirational resource, but their basic system of counseling, both theory and methods, is transferred unaltered from secular psychology.... Some Christian psychotherapists use few Scriptures; others use many. But frequency of citation is much less important than the way passages are used—or misused—and in the vast majority of cases the passages cited are completely misused. There is a dearth of contextualized exegesis (a critical interpretation of a text) and an abundance of eisegesis (interpreting a text by reading one's own ideas into it). Biblical counseling is committed to letting God speak for Himself through His Word, and to handling the Word of Truth rightly (2 Tim. 2:15).[4]

Powlison has attempted to address the evangelical psychotherapeutic establishment, asking that they would recognize

---

3. David Powlison, "Which Presuppositions? Secular Psychology and the Categories of Biblical Thought," *Journal of Psychology and Theology* 12, no. 4 (1984): 277–78.

4. David Powlison, "Frequently Asked Questions about Biblical Counseling," comp. and ed. Dennis Swanson, in *Introduction to Biblical Counseling: A Basic Guide to the Principles and Practice of Counseling*, ed. John MacArthur and Wayne Mack (Dallas: Word Publications), 363.

the radical nature of biblical presuppositions in counseling theory. He writes:

> A biblical view of presuppositions provides a sharply distinct alternative to any and all forms of secular thinking. It provides a truly coherent rationale for science. It provides a solid, biblical theoretical foundation for counseling people. It accounts for and appreciates the insights of psychology without losing sight of the pervasive distortion within each insight.[5]

In a lecture given at a counseling conference sponsored by the Christian Counseling and Educational Foundation, Bettler, who was then director of the CCEF and a faculty member at Westminster Theological Seminary, urged that "one of the signs that the movement called biblical counseling has been a success is that we have disagreements!" Bettler maintains that different styles and emphases should not be dismissed as less biblical than others. He asks, "To what irreducible commitments must you adhere in order to deserve the title 'biblical'?" His answer is to follow the historical model of establishing confessions of faith to define the parameters of biblical orthodoxy. With specific reference to the place of the past in the life of a counselee, Bettler states:

> I want us to do the dangerous job of drawing circles, drawing lines. Anybody within the circle is biblical, anybody outside the circle is not. That is a tough thing to do and there are dangers. Some of us might want to push the circles real wide; that tends towards liberalism.

---

5. Powlison, "Which Presuppositions?," 277–78.

Others of us might want to narrow the circles as tightly as we can; that tends toward becoming cultic or sectarian. We want to be biblical in dealing with the past. We want to search the Scripture to find commonality in this and other crucial counseling areas. Confession making is dangerous, but I believe it is essential. We have to do it in complete dependence upon the wisdom of the Holy Spirit. We need God to give us wisdom to be a community of learning so that we can learn from one another and stimulate one another unto good works.[6]

The fall 2000 issue of *The Journal of Biblical Counseling* features a series called "Affirmations & Denials: A Proposed Definition of Biblical Counseling" by Powlison. It is intended to be a draft of the type of confession-making referred to by Bettler. The following affirmations and denials speak to the issue of scriptural sufficiency:

> *We affirm* that the Bible is God's self-revelation in relation to His creatures, and, as such, truly explains people and situations.
>
> *We deny* that any other source of knowledge is authoritative for explaining people and situations.
>
> *We affirm* that the Bible, as the revelation of Jesus Christ's redemptive activity, intends to specifically guide and inform counseling ministry.
>
> *We deny* that any other source of knowledge is authoritative to equip us for the task of counseling people.

---

6. John Bettler, "Counseling and the Problem of the Past," *Journal of Biblical Counseling* 12, no. 2 (Winter 1994): 7.

> *We affirm* that wise counseling requires ongoing practical theological labor in order to understand Scripture, people and situations. We must continually develop our personal character, case-wise understanding of persons, pastoral skills, and institutional structures.
>
> *We deny* that the Bible intends to serve as an encyclopedia of proof texts containing all facts about people and the diversity of problems in living.[7]

Few, if any, nouthetic counselors would have difficulty with such statements. They uphold the sufficiency of Scripture and (although not explicitly stated as such) its superiority to general revelation. This is in contrast to many Christian psychologists who place each on an equal footing.[8] The draft confession also seeks to avoid the charge of proof texting. Differences arise among biblical counselors not so much in the commitment to biblical counseling, but in the application of the Scriptures in counseling. This includes avoiding defining biblical counseling by the term *nouthetic*.

---

7. David Powlison, "Affirmations & Denials: A Proposed Definition of Biblical Counseling," *The Journal of Biblical Counseling* 19, no. 1 (Fall 2000): 19.

8. Douglas Bookman, writing on the Scriptures and biblical counseling, faults the "two-book" view (general and special revelation) for misdefining both "general" and "revelation." "Revelation," he says, as classically understood, "is by definition nondiscoverable by human investigation or cognition.... Revelation is from God; thus it is by definition true and authoritative. To assign human discoveries to the category of general revelation is to imbue them with an aura of validity and consequent authority that they do not, indeed they cannot merit." Further, "general revelation is general not because it deals with a broad and nonspecific (that is, general) category of facts, but because it is accessible to all people of all time (that is, to people generally)." "The Scriptures and Biblical Counseling," in *Introduction to Biblical Counseling*, 72–76.

The Sufficiency of Nouthetic Counseling

In the early days of the CCEF, Bettler edited a newsletter called *Nouthetic Confrontation*. Later he changed the name to *Momentum*. He explained that nouthetic counseling was now gaining popularity, and it was time to move beyond the necessary image of confrontation in the movement's beginning to develop a more positive approach. In a later publication, he expressed concern that nouthetic counselors had a "tendency to twist...the Scripture to substantiate [its] conclusions." He accused them of sometimes making "the Scripture say something it never intended to say."[9] Bettler also echoes the common charge of illegitimate proof texting and emphasizing some biblical themes to the neglect of others.

Powlison uses the image of a fence surrounding the field of biblical counseling to describe the relationship between "the more authoritative, frankly remedial elements of counseling" and "the more mutual, ongoing encouraging elements." He writes (with lay counseling particularly in mind):

> Our goal is systematically biblical counseling, the ministry of God's truth in love. The "nouthetic part" of biblical counseling is the "fence." It is the backup mode of biblical counseling. It is for when the sheep leave the green pastures to wander out into the desert. The "paracletic" part of biblical counseling is the "field." It is the primary mode of biblical counseling, containing all the mutual edifying, encouraging, one anothering, nourishing, praying and loving that is the normal Christian

---

9. John Bettler, "Biblical Counseling: The Next Generation," *Journal of Pastoral Practice* 8, no. 4 (1987): 6.

life. It is as much a two way street as possible. It is as egalitarian as possible. It is as biblically "nondirective and client-centered" as possible.[10]

Elsewhere, Powlison has taken note of the criticism of Adams for choosing *noutheteō* rather than *parakaleō* as his defining term for biblical counseling. But he agrees with Adams that "the choice of words is indifferent—they can cover the same semantic field. Both words involve God's truth applied to lives, both words communicate love and concern, and both words communicate an appropriate directness and toughness."[11] But be that as it may, it is certain that Powlison, like Bettler, prefers to speak of "biblical" counseling more generically. He tends to avoid the negative connotations that have (rightly or wrongly) come to be associated with the term *nouthetic*.

At its 2013 annual conference, the National Association of Nouthetic Counselors (NANC), under the recently appointed leadership of Lambert, was asked to change its name to the Association of Certified Biblical Counselors (ACBC). One of the reasons given was that the movement is no longer national but international. But the main reason had to do with difficulties associated with having to explain what "nouthetic" means. Powlison endorsed the name change.[12]

---

10. David Powlison, "Crucial Issues in Contemporary Biblical Counseling," *Journal of Pastoral Practice* 9, no. 3 (1988): 67.

11. Powlison, "Biblical Counseling in the Twentieth Century," 51n.

12. David Powlison, "David Powlison Endorses the Name Change: Thoughts and Comments on the Name Change to ACBC from Powlison of CCEF," October 9, 2013, http://www.biblicalcounseling.com/blog/david-powlison-endorses-the-name-change.

However, Adams and those most closely associated with him continue to prefer the term *nouthetic*. They formed the Institute for Nouthetic Studies to specifically promote Adams's teaching and writing. Previously in the 1990s, Adams and others resigned from the board of the CCEF, which he had founded. This suggests that differences between the first and second generation of biblical counselors were over more than just nomenclature.[13]

Relation to Psychology and Psychiatry

Bettler distinguishes between "recycling" and the "integration" of theology and psychology popular among psychotherapists. His view is reflected in a course description from a brochure produced by the CCEF: "The course avoids their wholesale acceptance ('integration') which destroys Scripture's authority. It also avoids outright rejection, which robs the Christian counselor of the stimulus of secular insights. Instead a 'recycling' model is proposed to maintain the Bible's sufficiency as well as sharpen your understanding of biblical teaching."[14]

---

13. In a September 12, 2013, blog post written before the NANC (now ACBC) conference, Arms of the Institute for Nouthetic Studies argued with some justification that the term *biblical* is too broad in that counselors who take an integrationist approach, which nouthetic counselors reject as unbiblical, claim that what they are doing is "biblical" (Donn Arms, "Institute for Nouthetic Studies: Monthly Archives: September 2013," September 12, 2013, www.nouthetic.org/blog/?p=6206). Nevertheless, in a subsequent blog post, Arms admits that he was encouraged by the direction set by the conference for what he terms the NANC/ACBC (Donn Arms, "Institute for Nouthetic Studies: Monthly Archives: October 2013," October 29, 2013, www.nouthetic.org/blog/?p=6340).

14. In a discussion between Adams and Bettler, Bettler reminds Adams that it was Adams himself who first suggested the use of the term "recycling,"

Powlison evidences some ambivalence over the question of integration. In "Critiquing Modern Integrationists," he discusses various types of integration. Helpful material follows on how biblical Christians should view and use psychology and minister to the "psychologized." Using Calvin's analogy of the Scriptures as eyeglasses by which God corrects our sin-tainted vision, Powlison notes:

> The goal of biblically reinterpreting human experience—whether described by a counselee or a psychologist—is not "look how much we can learn from them." The goal is the ministry of the Word that concerns the soul. On the one hand, integrationists do not see that the pay-off of a valid biblical interaction with psychology must be the conversion of the psychologized. On the other hand, biblical counselors who do not do the hard work of reinterpreting error, standing it on its head, miss an opportunity for effective ministry.[15]

What, then, is the alternative to integration? In "Crucial Issues in Contemporary Biblical Counseling," Powlison writes:

> The relationship of presuppositionally consistent Christianity to secular culture is not simply one of rejection.

---

although he now says it "gives people the wrong idea." Bettler says that "Jay emphasizes the antithesis between belief and unbelief. I emphasize more the...recycling of error in the light of truth." Adams states, "I go back to Van Til's view. Go back, dig deep, examine presuppositions, attack them. Then reshape the whole business in light of Scriptural truth." David Powlison, "25 Years of Biblical Counseling: An Interview with Jay Adams and John Bettler," *Journal of Biblical Counseling* 12, no. 1 (Fall 1993): 8–13.

15. David Powlison, "Critiquing Modern Integrationists," *Journal of Biblical Counseling* 11, no. 3 (Spring 1993): 34.

Some Developments in Biblical Counseling

Half of what biblical presuppositions give us is a way to discern the lie that tries to make people think about themselves as autonomous from God.

But the other half of what biblical categories do is give us a way of appreciating, redeeming and reframing the culture of even the most godless men and women. We are, after all, even able to use the data gathered from godless counselees, reinterpreting their own perceptions back to them in biblical categories that turn their world inside out and upside down![16]

In his contributions to the book *Psychology & Christianity: Four Views*, Powlison defends biblical counseling and critiques three other approaches.[17] More recently, he has noted that while Christian psychologists in general became more explicitly biblical in the 1990s, "the 'biblical counselors' have also changed." He continues:

Their writings now evidence a broader scope of concerns and concepts than they had in the early 1970s. They have supplemented, developed, or even altered aspects of Adams's initial model. They are paying a great deal of attention to (1) intrapersonal dynamics such as motivation theory, self-evaluation, belief, and self-deception; (2) the impact of and response to varieties of suffering and socialization; (3) the compassionate, flexible, probing, and patient aspects of counseling methodology; (4) nuances in the interaction between Christian faith and the modern psychologies; (5) the practicalities of

---

16. Powlison, "Crucial Issues in Contemporary Biblical Counseling," 74.
17. Eric L. Johnson and Stanton L. Jones, *Psychology & Christianity: Four Views* (Downers Grove, Ill.: InterVarsity, 2000).

marital and familial communication; and (6) the cause and treatment of so-called addictions. The model of biblical counseling is now more detailed and comprehensive about any number of "psychological" matters.[18]

Still, while "the psychologists seem more biblical and the biblical counselors seem more psychological," Powlison continues to believe that "*the two visions are still fundamentally incompatible.*" However, he also believes that "our current situation is ripe for a fresh articulation of the issues.... The core question turns on the intent and scope of Scripture, the nature of pastoral theological work, and the degree of significance attached to what the church can appropriate from the world."[19]

In a 2012 article, Powlison adopts the term *redemption* in relation to secular psychology. This is surely a better and more clearly biblical term than Bettler's term *recycling*. Redeeming secular psychology involves, first, looking for the good. "Sectarian contentiousness only sees the bad, and does not produce redemption. But as in all the other mixed cases needing redemption, there is good in Psychology."[20] It is also necessary

---

18. David Powlison, "Cure of Souls & the Modern Psychotherapies," *Westminster Today* 4, no. 1 (Summer 2011): 9. In a much longer article by the same name, Powlison distinguishes between those who hold to VITEX (believing that secular psychologies "must make a vital external contribution in the construction of a Christian model of personality, change, and counseling") and COMPIN ("the Christian faith contains comprehensive internal resources to enable us to construct" a counseling model). See Powlison, *Biblical Counseling Movement*, appendix 4. (The reference to VIREX and COMPIN begins on page 275.)

19. Powlison, "Cure of Souls," 9.

20. David Powlison, "How Does Scripture Teach Us to *Redeem* Psychology?," *The Journal of Biblical Counseling* 26, no. 3 (2012): 19.

to identify what is wrong. "Compromising syncretism only sees the good, and does not produce redemption.... Fair minded judgment sees both the good and the bad, and offers something comprehensively better."[21] Powlison references Psalm 31 as an example of the true insight necessary for redemption.

> The psychological riches revealed are "by the way," a secondary spin-off from primary purposes. By revealing the true God in relation to his creatures, the Bible primarily intends to give us a new orientation and direction. Therefore, in a sense, Psalm 31 performs a psychotherapeutic intervention. It changes you, if you have ears to hear. This has huge implications for how Christian faith redeems the modern psychologies.[22]

Redemption of psychology involves addressing causality in human behavior. Powlison notes:

> Scientific researchers offer bare acknowledgement of a fact: all human beings operate with intentions.... But they sidestep the question of how to interpret this fact, because intentions can't be measured....
>
> Personality theorists go a step further and try to figure out the inner workings....
>
> Psychotherapists take a step further.... They hope to change what is troubling and destructive, so they must grapple hand-to-hand with what makes a person tick, whether or not they understand what that is.

---

21. Powlison, "How Does Scripture Teach Us to *Redeem* Psychology?," 19–20.

22. Powlison, "How Does Scripture Teach Us to *Redeem* Psychology?," 23.

> Typically, they assert the possibility of life-determining, volitional control....
>
> Unlike the scientific researchers, Christian truth reasons that the human factor is a decisive element in the complex of final causation....
>
> Unlike the personality theorists, Christian truth reasons that the deep motivating impulses of the human heart are not givens, but can and must be radically changed....
>
> Unlike the pragmatic people-helpers [i.e., psychotherapists], Christian truth reasons that human will is not free when it comes to the decisive life and death choices....
>
> Christian faith knows that by nature we are psychologically enslaved to instinctive desires of body and mind.[23]

But far more important than accurate self-knowledge is the awareness that "by the intervening grace of our merciful Redeemer we are truly forgiven...[and] decisively set free to want other things than what used to obsess us.... A secular psychotherapy, by definition, excludes such self-knowledge, such struggle, such transformation, and such joy."[24] In summary:

> What does it look like for psychology to be redeemed? Not a shred of valid information is lost, no skills in loving are forfeited, no hard questions are ducked. Rather, whatever was known is enriched and changed by being seen in a new and true light—and reams of

---

23. Powlison, "How Does Scripture Teach Us to *Redeem* Psychology?," 25–26.

24. Powlison, "How Does Scripture Teach Us to *Redeem* Psychology?," 27.

previously neglected information become available for the first time. Whatever was done skillfully is taken to an entirely different level when it is embedded in the purposes of Christ's redemptive love....

We redeem psychology as we learn to think theologically and redemptively about issues of life and death importance. We redeem psychology as we bring Scripture and Christian faith to bear in the psychological work of self-knowing, of knowing others, of making sense of our lives, and of participating in transformation—as individuals and all together—into the image of Jesus.[25]

Edward Welch (another faculty member and counselor at CCEF) does not deal so much with the sufficiency of Scripture or the integration of Scripture and psychology at a theoretical level. Rather, his interests are more in application, especially with the psychiatric study of the brain. His criticisms of secular psychologies and Christianized versions of them are very much along the lines of nouthetic orthodoxy.[26] But, because he is careful to discern what can be legitimately learned, his criticisms are all the more compelling. The title of one of Welch's books expresses his approach well: *Blame It on the Brain? Distinguishing Chemical Imbalances, Brain Disorders, and Disobedience*. Following a biblical study of the mind-body relationship, the book moves on to a section titled "Brain Problems Seen through the Lens of Scripture." Under the heading "The Brain Did It," two chapters are devoted to

---

25. Powlison, "How Does Scripture Teach Us to *Redeem* Psychology?," 27.
26. Edward T. Welch, *When People Are Big and God Is Small: Overcoming Peer Pressure, Codependency, and the Fear of Man* (Phillipsburg, N.J.: P&R, 1997), 139–51.

dementia associated with Alzheimer's disease and head injury from accidents. Here the goal is to provide "a method for approaching physical problems and gaining experience in distinguishing issues of the heart from physical weakness." Next come chapters on depression and attention deficit disorder in a section titled "Maybe the Brain Did It." Finally, homosexuality and alcoholism are studied as examples of "The Brain Didn't Do It."[27]

Welch offers the insightful observation that the brain can reveal what is in the heart. Thus, for instance, in the case of a hitherto morally upright Alzheimer's patient who begins to use crude and lustful language, he is no longer able to disguise the state of his heart as he once was.[28] In each area of application, Welch stresses the need to first of all "get information" and then "distinguish between spiritual and physical symptoms." This, in turn, leads to addressing heart issues and maximizing remaining strengths on the one hand, while correcting or minimizing weaknesses on the other. Thus, in his discussion of depression, Welch notes, "If depression consisted solely of spiritual problems, there would be no reason to talk about medication and other physical treatments. But depression does have physical symptoms. Therefore, medical treatment might be helpful to ease or erase the physical symptoms of depression (and those of other psychiatric problems)."[29]

In his *Counselor's Guide to the Brain and Its Disorders: Knowing the Difference between Disease and Sin*, Welch provides

---

27. Edward Welch, *Blame It on the Brain?* (Phillipsburg, N.J.: P&R, 1998).
28. Welch, *Blame It on the Brain?*, 67, 78–79.
29. Welch, *Blame It on the Brain?*, 125.

a somewhat more technical treatment of the uses and abuses of medication.[30] Elsewhere, contrary to Adams's approach, which encourages the counselor to assume a sin connection in the absence of clear evidence to the contrary, Welch cautions that to "reduce a person's suffering to the consequences of their own sin, especially when we don't have clear knowledge of the situation, is unbiblical and potentially destructive."[31]

This leads to another caution in which Welch's approach differs from Adams's. Welch writes, "To the degree that depression is, in fact, a form of suffering, then we have no biblical guarantee that it will be eradicated from our lives. We do have something close to a biblical promise that suffering, and therefore depression, will be lightened as we grow in Christ, but lightened does not mean depression-free."[32]

No careful reader of Welch comes away with the impression that he is soft on sin. Rather, precisely because he is so careful to distinguish between heart and brain issues, his treatment of the heart is all the more thorough and penetrating. His treatments of homosexuality and alcoholism are especially helpful in this regard.

---

30. Edward T. Welch, *Counselor's Guide to the Brain and Its Disorders: Knowing the Difference between Disease and Sin* (Grand Rapids: Zondervan, 1991).

31. Edward T. Welch, "Understanding Depression," *Journal of Biblical Counseling* 18, no. 2 (Winter 2000): 13. Welch has also written a book-length study on this subject: *Depression: A Stubborn Darkness* (Greensboro, N.C.: New Growth Press, 2004).

32. Edward T. Welch, "Helping Those Who Are Depressed," *Journal of Biblical Counseling* 18, no. 2 (Winter 2000): 27.

Means and Methods of Behavioral Change

When it comes to the actual process of helping people change behaviorally in a biblical manner, both Welch and Powlison make substantial use of two important categories. The first and most pervasive is what they call "idols of the heart." A second related insight is that people both sin and are sinned against. Both of these concepts go beyond simply identifying sinful behavior and calling for repentance.

Powlison articulated his approach in "Idols of the Heart and 'Vanity Fair.'" This proved to be a seminal work in the development of biblical counseling. For instance, in her 2001 book *Idols of the Heart: Learning to Long for God Alone*, Elyse Fitzpatrick credits Powlison with "reconfiguring" her thinking about idolatry.[33] Timothy Keller's introduction to *Counterfeit Gods* is called "The Idol Factory" and contains this statement: "The Bible's answer [to why we lose sight of what is right] is that the human heart is an 'idol factory.'"[34] Although he does not reference him here, Keller does include Powlison's article in his bibliography. Writing in 2009, Keller notes that the use of "idolatry as a major category for psychological and sociological analysis has been gaining steam in the last fifteen years in the academic world."[35] He references several academic works, both Jewish and Christian.

---

33. Elyse Fitzpatrick, *Idols of the Heart: Learning to Love God Alone* (Phillipsburg, N.J.: P&R, 2001), 11. Fitzpatrick, with Howard Eyrich, has also contributed a chapter on this subject to MacDonald, Kellemen, and Viars, *Christ-Centered Biblical Counseling*, 339–50.

34. Timothy Keller, *Counterfeit Gods: The Empty Promises of Money, Sex, and Power, and the Only Hope That Matters* (New York: Riverhead Trade Books, 2011), xiv.

35. Keller, *Counterfeit Gods*, 175n5.

Powlison's "Idols of the Heart and 'Vanity Fair'" is a discussion of the relationship between the biblical emphasis on idolatry and the psychological question of how to "make sense of the myriad significant factors which shape and determine human behavior."[36] While idolatry most often emerges in the context of worshiping physical images and false gods, Scripture also claims the problem is internal, as in Ezekiel 14:1–8. The first great commandment to love God with heart, soul, mind, and strength also demonstrates the essential "inwardness" of the law regarding idolatry. "The language of love, trust, fear, hope, seeking, serving—terms describing a relationship to the true God—is continually utilized in the Bible to describe our false loves, false trusts, false fears, false hopes, false pursuits, false masters."[37]

If *idolatry* is the characteristic Old Testament word for "our drift from God," then *desires* is the New Testament equivalent. "The New Testament language of problematic 'desires' is a dramatic expansion of the tenth commandment, which forbids coveting...[and] internalizes the problem of sin, making it 'psychodynamic.'" Powlison continues:

> [It] lays bare the grasping and demanding nature of the human heart, as Paul powerfully describes it in Romans 7. Interestingly (and unsurprisingly) the New Testament merges the concept of idolatry and the concept of inordinate, life-ruling desires. Idolatry becomes a

---

36. David Powlison, "Idols of the Heart and 'Vanity Fair,'" *The Journal of Biblical Counseling* 13, no. 2 (Winter 1995): 35.

37. Powlison, "Idols of the Heart," 36.

problem of the heart, a metaphor for human lust, craving, yearning and greedy demand.[38]

The Bible also treats idolatry as "a central feature of the social context, 'the world,' which shapes and molds us." Like "Vanity Fair" in John Bunyan's *Pilgrim's Progress*, it can be seen as "portraying the interaction of powerful, enticing and intimidating social shapers of behavior with the self-determining tendencies of Christian's own heart."[39]

Idols allure us from both within and without. This fact "has provocative implications for contemporary counseling questions." For instance, "the life patterns often labelled 'codependency' are more precisely and penetratingly understood as instances of 'co-idolatry.'"[40] The idolatry motif helps relate three factors that enter into counseling situations: people are responsible for their own problems; their problems are shaped by external influences including traumatic influences such as loss or victimization; and problematic behavior is often driven by deep-seated motives of which a person may be "almost wholly unaware."[41]

Powlison asserts, "The Bible's view of man—both individual and social life—alone holds these things together." This is because human motivation is always "with respect to God." The biblical theme of idolatry provides a "penetrating tool" for understanding both the "springs of and inducements to" sinful behavior. Powlison writes:

---

38. Powlison, "Idols of the Heart," 36.
39. Powlison, "Idols of the Heart," 36.
40. Powlison, "Idols of the Heart," 37.
41. Powlison, "Idols of the Heart," 38.

Some Developments in Biblical Counseling

> The causes of particular sins, whether "biological drives," "psychodynamic forces from within," "socio-cultural conditioning from without," or "demonic temptation and attack from without" can be truly comprehended through the lens of idolatry. Such comprehension plows the field for Christian counseling to become Christian in deed as well as name, to become ministry of the many-faceted good news of Jesus Christ.[42]

"What happens to the gospel when idolatry themes are not grasped?" Powlison asks:

> Where "the Gospel" is shared, it comes across something like this: "God accepts *you* just as *you* are. God has unconditional love for you." This is not the biblical Gospel, however. God's love is not Rogerian unconditional positive regard writ large. A need theory of motivation—rather than an idolatry theory—bends the Gospel solution into "another gospel" which is essentially false.
>
> The Gospel is better than unconditional love. The Gospel says, God accepts you just as Christ is.... God never accepts me "as-I-am." He accepts me "as-I-am-in-Jesus Christ." The center of gravity is different. The true Gospel does not allow God's love to be sucked into the vortex of my soul's lust for acceptability and worth in and of myself. Rather, it radically decenters people—what the Bible calls "fear of the Lord" and "faith"—to look outside themselves.[43]

---

42. Powlison, "Idols of the Heart," 41.
43. Powlison, "Idols of the Heart," 49.

Christian counselors with a "psychologizing drift" are susceptible to the above distortion of the gospel. However, Christian counselors with "moralistic tendencies" have a different set of problems. Christ's forgiveness is "typically applied simply to behavioral sins." The content of the gospel "is usually more orthodox than the content of the psychologized Gospel, but the scope of application is truncated." Those with "psychologizing tendencies" at least notice our "inner complexities and outer sufferings, though they distort both systemically." In some ways, "the moralizing tendency represents an inadequate grip on the kind of 'bad news' which [Powlison's] article [explores]."[44]

Powlison's examples of "moralistic tendencies" are the "let go and let God" and "total yieldedness" approaches. These are like "a single act of first-blessing or second-blessing housecleaning" with little sense of the "patient *process* of inner renewal."[45] These examples do not apply to Adams or nouthetic counselors in general who stress progressive sanctification. But Powlison has elsewhere conceded that the criticisms of "moralism" and "behaviorism" hit home there also.[46]

Welch's treatment of these themes is most thoroughly and helpfully developed in *When People Are Big and God Is Small*. However, while we will refer to this work, it is sufficient for our present purposes to summarize his use of these

---

44. Powlison, "Idols of the Heart," 49.

45. Powlison, "Idols of the Heart," 49–50.

46. "We depart from the Bible if we ignore motives and drift towards an externalistic view of man. The caricature that we are behavioristic may indeed be true more often than we like to admit. The Bible itself tells us behavior has reasons." Powlison, "Crucial Issues in Contemporary Biblical Counseling," 56.

concepts in his chapter "Codependency and the Cult of Self," contributed to the book *Power Religion*, edited by Michael Scott Horton. Here, after outlining the popular codependent movement, Welch asks, "If we are not to use the categories of 'self-esteem,' 'unmet needs,' 'codependency,' and the notion of the basically good 'child within,' what descriptions rise out of biblical categories?" He answers:

> According to Scripture, we are sinners by birth (original sin) and sinners by choice. Sin is a condition arising from a fallen nature that is hostile to God, and this condition produces personal choices and actions that are sinful. But because we are all sinners, there is a third element: although we are sinners by birth and sinners by choice, we are also sinned against. There is a legitimate place in Scripture given to the idea that we both victimize others and are ourselves victims of the sinful actions of other people and institutions.[47]

Next, we come to the concept of idolatry. "The characteristic strategy of idolatry is to take something that is fine in itself and exalt it so that it rules the person." Consider the desire to be loved, which is normally a "blessing." "However, when it moves from godly desire to ruling passion or need, it is evidence of the sinful tendency to serve other gods, all ultimately in an effort to worship oneself." It often "takes the mode of a quiet, unspoken conviction" that because God does not meet all one's needs, one can divide one's allegiance and trust in idols instead of God. Paradoxically, though, when we

---

47. Ezekiel 37 is supplied as an example.

offer ourselves to idols, we become their slaves. "That is idolatry: seeking to control, but being controlled."[48]

Welch and Powlison are both critical of all "needs" theories, including those of Crabb, whom they nevertheless recognize as being closer to their own position than others (e.g., Minirth-Meier, who adopt the codependency model). Although appreciative of Crabb in several respects, Powlison indicts him for having affinities "with secular theories which make drives, needs, instincts, wishes or impulses the fundamental and animating givens of human nature. Rather than seeing human beings as fundamentally proactive worshipers, Crabb's system understands people to be motivated by what Abraham Maslow termed deficiency needs."[49] Welch, likewise, finds Crabb's change of terminology from "needs" to "deep longings" to be unsatisfactory. He is concerned that this means "we have a longings problem that is at least as deep as our sin problem."[50] Welch believes that instead of finding the source of psychological needs in our creation in the image of God, we should look for it in the fall where "the direction of the human heart became oriented not toward God but toward self.... Is it possible that the '*I want*' of Adam is the first expression of psychological needs? Is it that psychological yearnings come when we refuse to love God and receive his love?"[51]

Adams is among those who endorsed Welch's book. He stated, "I know of no other book that so fully deals with

---

48. Edward T. Welch, "Codependency and the Cult of Self," in *Power Religion*, ed. Michael Scott Horton (Chicago: Moody Press, 1992), 233–36.
49. Powlison, "Larry Crabb and Biblical Counseling," 9.
50. Welch, *When People Are Big and God Is Small*, 146.
51. Welch, *When People Are Big and God Is Small*, 148.

the fear of man and its baneful effects. It is must reading for counselors who care to help others do something about it." Clearly, by implication, Adams sees Welch's work as an extension of his own. However, it is the attention to inner motivation and the much greater recognition of the effects of being sinned against that set Welch's (as well as Powlison's) work apart from Adams's. As much as anything, this comes across in an understanding of people's problems that at least gives the impression of greater empathy. Compare, for instance, Adams's rather harsh description of a victimized child as quoted earlier with Welch's description of the effects of destructive speech as well as acts:

> How, I wonder does cruel speech affect children? I know that children are immensely resilient, and I am not suggesting that one word will scar a child for life, but the Bible indicates that reckless words pierce like a sword (Prov. 12:18). The Bible never minimizes the effect of sinful words. It exposes them as firebrands that leave wounds that can go to the deepest parts of our being. They stand in stark contrast to the words of compassion and healing that the Lord offers such victims. I have seen children who have been crushed by the words of another. I have watched as some of them gradually become more reticent and withdrawn. They looked as if they were scared, always defensive and hypervigilent, as if they were in a battle. Is the sin of other people leaving them prone to a heightened version of the fear of man? In some cases, yes.[52]

---

52. Welch, *When People Are Big and God Is Small*, 53.

Sometimes it is the tone, as much as anything else, that communicates understanding and the desire to help.

In "Is Biblical-Nouthetic Counseling Legalistic? Reexamination of a Biblical Theme," Welch first defines legalism as "the prideful motives and purposes behind the legalistic tendency that is resident in everyone." He shows how legalism and slavery are companions. Then he notes that, conversely, "faith is inseparable from freedom and sonship." The apostle Paul contrasts sonship to the slavery of legalism. Slaves under the law have now received the full privileges of sonship. Therefore, "you are no longer a slave, but a son, and if a son, then an heir of God through Christ" (Gal. 4:7)." The juxtaposition is dramatic. The experience of the adopted child includes:

> An unfailing relationship characterized by love;
> Acceptance based on the performance of Christ rather than our own;
> Forgiveness rather than repayment;
> Being known and understood;
> The promise of even greater things (an eternal inheritance) so there is no need to worry about the future;
> Transformation into the image of the Father by the indwelling Spirit of sonship; therefore, there is power to change.[53]

---

53. Edward T. Welch, "Is Biblical-Nouthetic Counseling Legalistic? Reexamination of a Biblical Theme," *Journal of Pastoral Practice* 11, no. 1 (1992): 17.

"Turning away from sin," Welch notes, "is undeniably part of obedience. But it is a response to the gospel (the death and resurrection of Jesus) not commensurate with it."[54]

In *When People Are Big and God Is Small*, Welch deals extensively with the biblical concept of the fear of God as the antidote to the fear of man. He ends the book with a chapter titled "The Conclusion of the Matter: Fear God and Keep His Commandments." This is preceded by separate chapters on loving our enemies and neighbors and loving our brothers and sisters. These are familiar themes in nouthetic counseling. But before getting to them, Welch has a chapter titled "Delight in the God Who Fills Us." Here he spends time on the biblical story of Hosea's love for his unfaithful bride, Gomer. This illustrates God's love for His unfaithful people, Israel, and Christ's love for those for whom He gave His life:

> Our God no longer calls us slaves. Through Jesus, he calls us friends, children, and his bride. Through his Spirit, he gives us the greatest gift we could ever have. He gives us himself. He says, "I am with you" (cf. John 14:27–28). "Never will I leave you; never will I forsake you." So we can say with confidence, "The Lord is my helper: I will not be afraid. What can man do to me?" (Heb. 13:5–6).[55]

All biblical counselors, Adams included, would endorse the above. However, it is the seeming lack of attention to this powerful biblical motivation that creates the impression of an imbalance in need of redress.

---

54. Welch, "Is Biblical-Nouthetic Counseling Legalistic?," 20.
55. Welch, *When People Are Big and God Is Small*, 179.

In his previously referenced work, Lambert notes:

> Biblical counselors have advanced the theological reflection of Adams about how to do ministry in two important ways. (1) They have brought about great development in an understanding of how to do ministry to people who are suffering as well as to people who are sinning.... (2) More contemporary biblical counselors have developed the movement with regard to motivational issues...the issue of why people do the things they do.[56]

The main part of Lambert's book is largely taken up with discussion of the two major developments noted above. When it comes to the "idols of the heart" motif, Lambert suggests it needs further development. He devotes a chapter to the subject. Following a brief survey of idolatry in the Old and New Testaments, Lambert argues:

> The main problem sinful people have is not idols of the heart per se. The main problem certainly involves idols and is rooted in the heart, but the idols are manifestations of the deeper problem. The heart-problem is self-exaltation, and idols are two or three steps removed.... Even though idols change from culture to culture and from individual to individual within a culture, the fundamental problem of humanity has not changed since Genesis 3: sinful people want—more than anything in the world—to be like God.[57]

---

56. Lambert, *Biblical Counseling Movement*, 45.
57. Lambert, *Biblical Counseling Movement*, 148.

Citing Powlison's article "Idols of the Heart and 'Vanity Fair,'" Lambert observes that Powlison seems to recognize a need for development along Lambert's own lines. Lambert writes, "The motivational distinction being made here between specific idols and the sinful self-exalting heart is in many ways subtle, but the distinction has great practical relevance for counseling, which is seen in at least seven ways."[58] These are a better understanding of pride, people, sin, repentance, compassionate counseling, protection against "idol hunts," and protection against introspection.

In an extensive review of Lambert's book, Winston Smith, a CCEF faculty member, suggests that "advancement isn't so much a matter of clarifying the sinful core of idolatry but of exploring the many ways that the Bible asks us to explore our brokenness and need for redemption."[59] Powlison sees the concern about "idol hunts" to be a misreading and misapplication of his article. He reprinted it in *The Journal of Biblical Counseling* in 2013, with an introductory clarification:

> Often I've heard this article referred to in shorthand as "Idols of the Heart." But my title intentionally also names and extensively discusses "Vanity Fair," by which I mean the situational forces that beset us. The article is as much about looking around as it is about looking in the mirror…. If I go on an "idol hunt" into myself, I become intensely introspective and analytical. Similarly, if I go on an "idol hunt" into you, I try to read your mind, as if

---

58. Lambert, *Biblical Counseling Movement*, 150.
59. Winston Smith, "The Biblical Counseling Movement after Adams," February 2012, http://www.reformation21.org/shelf-life/the-biblical-counseling-movement-after-adams.php.

I could peer into your heart, as if I had the right to judge you. Idol hunts of any kind forget that knowing ourselves and others is not an end in itself. Accurate knowledge of our need leads us directly away from ourselves and into the mercies of God for us and for others.[60]

Not surprisingly, Adams is one who expresses concern about "idol hunts." Indeed, he takes exception to the very term "idols of the heart." He points out that God alone knows the heart. "Nowhere [in Scripture] is searching another's heart set forth as a counseling construct."[61] Although Powlison does not mention Adams (or Lambert) by name, he likely had such criticisms in mind when he stated that his article "is not teaching a counseling methodology.... It only seeks to bring clarity amid the conflicting theories about why people do what they do."[62]

Once a counselee's problems have been properly and biblically analyzed, it is time to point him to the solution, which all biblical counselors would agree is found in the gospel of Christ. But once again, there appears to be a difference at least in emphasis among biblical counselors. Some, such as Adams, having secured a verbal profession of faith in Christ, move directly to the obedience demanded of believers. Others such as Powlison and Welch spend more time on the gospel itself as good news for those who suffer. Welch is particularly helpful here in distinguishing between the hope of the gospel and

---

60. David Powlison, "Revisiting Idols of the Heart and Vanity Fair," *Journal of Biblical Counseling* 27, no. 3 (2013): 40–42.

61. Jay E. Adams, "The Heart of the Matter," May 7, 2012, http://www.nouthetic.org/blog/?p=792.

62. Powlison, "Revisiting Idols of the Heart and Vanity Fair," 38.

the perception of legalism of which nouthetic counselors are often accused.

Sin, Sickness, and Satan

In the article referenced above, Powlison observes that if he had thought to impose a longer title on readers, he could have called the original "Idols of the Heart, Vanity Fair, and the Prince of Darkness." He goes on to explain why he did not do so, since any piece of writing "occurs against a backdrop.... This article primarily holds a running conversation with the motivational theories of the psychological sciences and therapies."[63] Powlison cautions against too great an emphasis on the devil. However, as we have seen, he does point out the "demonological" as well as the "psychological" and "sociological" dimension of idolatrous motivation.

Powlison has also written a helpful book titled *Power Encounters*. Here, he provides a biblically balanced treatment of the role of Satan—including demon possession—in human suffering and spiritual warfare, in both situational evils (outer man suffering) and the in-working power (temptation) of moral evil. He argues that there is no biblical command to cast out demons as Jesus and His apostles did. Jesus treated moral and situational evil differently. Situational evils which Jesus relieved through exorcism are included among the sick whom He healed (Matt. 4:23–25; Luke 6:18; 7:21; 8:2; 9:42; 13:11–13). Moral evil was dealt with both in the Gospels and Epistles by what Powlison calls the "classic mode" of spiritual warfare—evangelism, discipleship, and personal growth. He

---

63. Powlison, "Revisiting Idols of the Heart and Vanity Fair," 40.

notes that John Nevius, a Presbyterian missionary to China in the nineteenth century, "is often considered the founder of modern practical demonology because of his book *Demon Possession and Allied Themes*. He reported hundreds of cases of demon possession among the Chinese but used the classic mode to deliver them."[64] Thus, Powlison would differ with some of Adams's critics, such as Lloyd-Jones, who advocate exorcism for the demonically possessed. However, he does recognize, more than Adams appears to, the possibility of direct (rather than indirect) demonic activity in those whose suffering might lead them to seek the help of a biblical counselor.[65]

It is significant, as Powlison notes, that when Paul speaks of believers being engaged in spiritual warfare, he does not speak of exorcism. Rather, Paul speaks of truth, righteousness, the gospel, faith, salvation, Scripture, and prayer (see Eph. 6:10–18). Nonetheless, the reality is that our struggle is against the spiritual forces of evil and the devil who prowls around as a roaring lion looking for someone to devour (1 Peter 5:8). Sensitivity to his power and influence should at least leave open the possibility of satanic oppression as the primary cause of suffering, either mentally in some cases or like it was in Job's physical and emotional suffering.

Chapter 4

Biblical and Puritan Counseling

Powlison, Welch, and others make extensive use of the "idols of the heart" motif. While their primary references are to Scripture, the language also suggests the influence of the Puritans. E. Brooks Holifield writes in his *History of Pastoral Care in America*, "The Puritan pastor, especially in the seventeenth century, became a specialist in the cure of the idolatrous heart. He analyzed motives, evaluated feelings, sought to discern hidden intentions and to direct inward consent."[1]

Welch refers to Calvin rather than the Puritans. But Powlison gives more explicit recognition of Puritan emphases when, in discussing questions of the integration of theology and psychology, he notes that in the century after Jonathan Edwards (1703–1758), "American Protestantism divided roughly into three: Reformed orthodoxy, revivalism, proto-liberalism. None of these engaged the issues of the human heart in a detailed way."[2] Powlison goes on to show how

---

1. E. Brooks Holifield, *A History of Pastoral Care in America: From Salvation to Self-Realization* (Nashville: Abingdon Press), 23.

2. David Powlison, "Integration or Inundation?," in *Power Religion*, 202. Strictly speaking, Edwards lived after the Puritan era, but is considered to be a representative of that tradition.

secular psychology filled a vacuum, dealing with the intricacies of "motivation, defensiveness, interpersonal conflict, communication, problem solving, anger, anxiety, depression, guilt, the grieving process, parenting, sexuality, addictions." But those issues, says Powlison, are "precisely the cognitive and practical domain of the Bible itself.... The Bible is centrally about domains in which secular psychologists have laid claim to truth and competency."[3]

In "Biblical Counseling in the Twentieth Century," Powlison notes that "English-speaking believers have a long history of case-wise pastoral care. Many of the greatest Protestant writers are marked by an ability to bring Scripture to bear sensitively on various 'cases.'"[4] Here he mentions four classics, three from the Puritan era: Thomas Brooks's *Precious Remedies against Satan's Devices*; Richard Baxter's *A Christian Directory*; John Bunyan's *The Pilgrim's Progress*; and the post-Puritan Jonathan Edwards's *A Treatise Concerning Religious Affections*.

This chapter of Powlison's in *Introduction to Biblical Counseling* is preceded by Ken L. Sarles's, titled "The English Puritans: A Historical Paradigm of Biblical Counseling." Sarles discusses the Puritan views of Scripture, God, man, and sin. He then asks why we should use the Puritan approach today. It is "because the spiritual, devotional, theocentric commitment, and personal integrity of the Puritans reflects biblical reality and is worthy of present-day evangelical emulation." How, then, should we use the Puritan approach?

---

3. Powlison, "Integration or Inundation?," 204.
4. Powlison, "Biblical Counseling in the Twentieth Century," 44.

> [It is] by applying the theological truths they employed to the psychological presuppositions of our own day. Their view of how sin dominates the life provides the key to understanding addictive behavior. Their God-centeredness establishes the framework for a proper approach to self-image.... The defining characteristic of Puritanism was the stress on the sanctified life. Whether in the area of counseling, or any other area of Christian life and ministry, the Puritans challenge us today, more than any other generation in the history of the Church, by their absolute commitment to integrity between action and belief.[5]

Sarles evidences considerable dependence on an article by Timothy Keller, who, before he became famous as a popular author and pastor of Redeemer Presbyterian Church in New York, was associate professor of practical theology at Westminster Seminary in Philadelphia. He is still associated with that institution, where the modern biblical counseling movement was born. In the twentieth-anniversary issue of *The Journal of Pastoral Practice*, Keller contributed an article titled "Puritan Resources for Biblical Counseling." The article begins with this summary:

> The works of the Puritans are a rich resource for biblical counselors because:
> 1. The Puritans were committed to the functional authority of Scripture. For them it was the comprehensive manual for dealing with all problems of the heart.

---

5. Ken L. Sarles, "The English Puritans: A Historical Paradigm of Biblical Counseling," in *Introduction to Biblical Counseling*, 42–43.

2. The Puritans developed a sophisticated and sensitive system of diagnosis for personal problems, distinguishing a variety of physical, spiritual, temperamental and demonic causes.

3. The Puritans developed a remarkable balance in their treatment because they were not invested in any one "personality theory" other than biblical teaching about the heart.

4. The Puritans were realistic about difficulties of the Christian life, especially conflicts with remaining, indwelling sin.

5. The Puritans looked not just at behavior but at underlying root motives and desires. Man is a worshipper; all problems grow out of "sinful imagination" or idol manufacturing.

6. The Puritans considered the essential spiritual remedy to be belief in the gospel, used in both repentance and the development of proper self-understanding.[6]

Noting that the Puritans were the first "Protestant school of Biblical Counseling," Keller quotes J. I. Packer as stating that "the Puritans…were strongest just where evangelical Christians today are weakest.… Here were men of outstanding intellectual power, in whom the mental habits fostered by sober scholarship were linked with a flaming zeal for God and a minute acquaintance with the human heart." Keller continues, "Today's biblical scholars don't understand the human heart, Packer says, while our counselors don't know

---

6. Timothy J. Keller, "Puritan Resources for Biblical Counseling," *Journal of Pastoral Practice* 9, no. 3 (1988): 11. See also Mark Deckard, *Helpful Truth in Past Places: The Puritan Practice of Biblical Counseling* (Fearn, Ross-shire: Christian Focus, 2010).

the Scripture. But the Puritans were an entire generation of men who combined these two strengths."[7]

After developing the six points above by surveying the contributions of Thomas Brooks, Richard Baxter, John Owen, Richard Sibbes, Stephen Charnock, Jonathan Edwards, and William Gurnall, Keller ends with the following implications for today:

> The Puritans probably would not find themselves fitting in comfortably to most of the existing "schools" in the evangelical counseling field. They would probably find some counselors overly concerned to "raise self-esteem" when man's main problem is self-worship. Yet, on the other hand they would not be in agreement with those who completely ignore or even reject the importance of reprogramming the self-understanding through the penetration of gospel truth. They probably would find many biblical counselors are being far too superficial in their treatment of problems by merely calling for surface repentance and behavioral change. But they also would be quite uncomfortable with the "inner healing" approaches which virtually ignore behavior and the need for mortification. In fact, the Puritans would be quite unhappy talking about people's "unmet needs" because at bottom they believed a man does not have abstract needs, only a necessity for worship....
>
> Above all, the Puritans' "spirit" would differ quite a bit from other counselors today. Most modern evangelical counselors simply lack the firmness, directness and

---

7. Keller, "Puritan Resources," 11. Cf. J. I. Packer, foreword to *Introduction to Puritan Theology: A Reader*, ed. Edward E. Hindson (Grand Rapids: Baker, 1976), 12. (Keller's reference for the Packer quote appears to be mistaken.)

urgency of the Puritans. Most of us talk less about sin than did our forefathers. But on the other hand, the Puritans amazingly were tender, encouraging, always calling the [counselees] to accept the grace of God and extremely careful not to call a problem "sin" unless it was analyzed carefully. One of their favorite texts was: "A bruised reed he will not break, and a smoking flax he will not quench" (Matthew 12:20).

When will we see their likes again?[8]

While the Puritans clearly took sin seriously as the root cause of human suffering, they also recognized that self-understanding was not limited to coming to terms with one's sinfulness. They took seriously the reality of satanic attack and made a clear distinction between Satan's temptations and our succumbing to these temptations. Brooks, for instance, recognized that depression can arise from a wounded or overscrupulous conscience as much as from a numb or seared conscience.[9]

Keller sees Baxter as a standard in terms of dealing with the complexities of human personality. He analyzes Baxter's sermon "What Are the Best Preservatives against Melancholy and Overmuch Sorrow?" and notes that Baxter discerns four causes of depression—sin, physiology, temperament, and demonic activity—which can exist in a variety of interrelationships.[10]

---

8. Keller, "Puritan Resources," 40.

9. Keller, "Puritan Resources," 13. Cf. Thomas Brooks, *Precious Remedies against Satan's Devices*, in *The Works of Thomas Brooks*, ed. Alexander B. Grosart (Edinburgh: Banner of Truth, 1980), 1:I.3; III.1, 2, 7.

10. Keller, "Puritan Resources," 15–16. Cf. Richard Baxter, "What Are the Best Preservatives against Melancholy and Overmuch Sorrow?," in *The*

Keller summarizes as follows:

> The Puritans' balanced understanding of the roots of personal problems is not mirrored in the pastoral practice of modern evangelicals. Most counselors tend to "major" in one of the factors mentioned by Baxter. Some will see personal sin as the cause of nearly all problems. Others have built a counseling methodology mainly upon an analysis of "transformed temperaments." Still others have developed "deliverance" ministries which see personal problems largely in terms of demonic activity. And of course, some evangelicals have adopted the whole "medical model" of mental illness, removing all "moral blame" from the patient, who needs not repentance but the treatment of a physician. But Baxter not only shows an objective openness to discovering any of these factors in diagnosis, he also expects usually to find all of them present. Any of the factors may be the main factor which must be dealt with first in order to deal with the others. So we see the sophistication of the Puritans as physicians of the soul. If anything the Puritans sometimes made distinctions unnecessarily.... But biblical counselors today, who sometimes are rightfully charged with being simplistic, could learn from the careful diagnostic methods of these fathers in the faith.[11]

Keller cites Charnock as one who used the "idols of the heart" theme. But he notes that Charnock was "by no means

---

Morning Exercises at Cripplegate (Wheaton, Ill.: Richard Owen Roberts, 1981), 3:264–65. See also Baxter's more extensive treatment of melancholy (depression) in *A Christian Directory*, in *The Practical Works of Richard Baxter* (Ligonier, Pa.: Soli Deo Gloria), 1:261–67.

11. Keller, "Puritan Resources," 18.

alone." Baxter outlined "great sins" or idolatries of pride, sensuality, materialism, hypocrisy, and man-pleasing. Owen "names self-elation (power-idolatry), sensuality (comfort-idolatry) and unbelief (self-will). Though the lists differ in length, the same basic analysis is held by most of the Puritan divines."[12]

Charnock's treatment of heart idolatry is helpfully related to the subject of self-love (a popular theme among contemporary counselors). He distinguishes between "natural self-love," such as the care of the body Paul refers to in Ephesians 5:29, and "carnal self-love," that is "natural self-love which has become 'criminal in excess' under the influence of sin." It is when we love ourselves more than God, and our interests center on ourselves. This form of self-love is idolatry. But then there is a "gracious self-love" produced by the Holy Spirit. "Charnock says a Christian was created for good works (Ephesians 2:10) and as he comes to see this as his true 'end' or purpose, he becomes well pleased with himself.... It is a state of peace and satisfaction that comes from a proper self-understanding that fits with our true nature as servants."[13]

The goal of Puritan counseling was to help counselees move from idolatrous self-love to gracious self-love. In this, the imagination played a crucial role. Unlike modern cognitive therapists who see "thinking" as fundamental to behavior and feeling, the Puritans went further and stressed that the thought that captures the imagination will control the emotions and will. Sinful imaginations must be replaced by

---

12. Keller, "Puritan Resources," 30–31.
13. Keller, "Puritan Resources," 29–31. Cf. Stephen Charnock, *Discourses Upon the Existence of God* (Grand Rapids: Baker, 1979), 1:136.

religious affections as our thinking is reprogrammed to be full of thoughts that reflect the truth of Philippians 4:8, "Whatever things are true, whatever things are noble, whatever things are just, whatever things are pure, whatever things are lovely, whatever things are of good report, if there is any virtue and if there is anything praiseworthy—meditate on these things."[14] This is fundamentally the work of the Holy Spirit, who uses prayer, meditation, and the application of Scripture to effect change that is more than behavioral and cognitive, "recognizing that the truth must penetrate to the heart for real growth to occur." This means that the imagination must be captured for Christ. "It is to live in holy consciousness of, to be melted by spiritual understanding of one's privileges and standing in Christ."[15]

The Puritans, Keller says, "provided balanced solutions not based on a particular 'personality theory.'" He writes:

> Many Christian counselors tend to mirror secular approaches that either focus their treatment largely on the feelings (such as the client-centered approach of Rogers), on the actions (such as the behavioral approach of Skinner and his kin) or on the 'thinking' (such as the rational-emotive therapies of Ellis and Beck). But the Puritans do not fit into any of these modern categories.[16]

Consider Brooks's *Precious Remedies against Satan's Devices*. Many of Brooks's remedies look similar to cognitive therapy.

---

14. Keller quotes from the NIV—"whatever is true, whatever is noble, whatever is right, whatever is admirable"—but omits "whatever is lovely."

15. Keller, "Puritan Resources," 34.

16. Keller, "Puritan Resources," 18.

He sees problems as "largely due to doctrinal distortions, to unbelief and lies that we believe about God and ourselves." Thus, he provides "passionate scriptural arguments to be thrust forcibly and constantly into the consciousness against the lies which are dominating the heart." Keller continues:

> [Brooks] constantly urges the reader to "dwell more upon" particular truths,...seeking to change the thinking in order to relieve anxiety, fear, depression. Yet he can also appear to be a behaviorist at times, calling people to change their pattern of living immediately. Brooks is not afraid to plumb deep for underlying motives and desires. He comforts. He takes emotional states seriously.

So is Brooks a behaviorist, a cognitive therapist, or a Rogerian?

> Of course the answer is: "none of the above".... He does not consider either "thinking" or "behavior" or "emotion" to be the most basic part of personality. Neither does he appear to have his own personality theory in which he inter-relates these components in a neat pattern of cause and effect. Instead he concentrates on the heart (a word Brooks uses interchangeably with the word soul). The "motions" of the heart are thoughts, feelings and actions. Problems develop when the heart operates in unbelief. Problems are solved when the truth of the Word is "presented" (Brooks' terminology) to the heart, and that means to the thoughts as well as the will and emotions. Brooks will tell a person to obey a truth instantly and at the same time to reflect and

dwell on it until the principle changes his thinking and feelings as well.[17]

Keller points to John Owen as most helpful in dealing with the problem of indwelling sin:

> To Owen the major difference between the believer and the non-believer is that the dominion of sin is broken (Romans 6). However, the influence of sin remains in the believer with its basic tendencies the same, though badly weakened. There are, then, two basic pastoral problems: to convince those under sin's dominion that they really are and to convince those not under sin's dominion that they really are not. Biblical counselors must be prepared to skillfully accomplish both tasks.
>
> What are the signs of the dominion of sin?... An openly licentious life shows the person to be under the dominion of sin, whatever he may claim. But Owen is quick to point out that dominion does not have to show itself in outward acts. A life of outward morality, an interest in Bible study, an enjoyment of religious duties and a repentance for outward sins (all these may be present and yet sin still be "reigning"). Sin is reigning when the "imagination" (i.e. the motives) of the heart are controlled by sin. The basic patterns of sinful imaginations are three, according to Owen: 1) "pride, self-elation, desire of power and greatness," 2) "sensuality and uncleanness of life" and 3) "unbelief, distrust, and hard thoughts of God"; self-centeredness, self-gratification and self-will.

---

17. Keller, "Puritan Resources," 19–20. Cf. Brooks, *Precious Remedies*, 1:1–166.

> While believers are not under the dominion of sin, they are still under the influence of it. It has real power; it remains in believers, though dethroned....
>
> How, then, can we tell the difference between the dominion of sin and remaining sin in the believer? Owen believed it was crucial for counselors to be able to tell the difference! The question is especially important because sin may become more violent and apparently stronger because it has been overthrown and is dying.
>
> Owen teaches first that the dominion of sin is seen in "hardness of heart." Believers are influenced by the power of sin but they are grieved over their sinful motives. The very grief and concern over their sin is a healthy sign that a person is not under sin's reign. Owen points out that real believers engage in "mortification": they recognize and work on sinful motives, rather than just noticing external behavior. "When the only restraints on sin are the consequences of the action, sin has dominion in the will."[18]

For those under the dominion of sin, the counseling approach is evangelism. These people need a clear presentation of the gospel so that they will see their sin as sin, not simply the pain that is the consequence of sin. The same, however, is true of those who, having believed the gospel, still struggle with indwelling sin. Among the directions Owen gives is that one must take sin not just to the law but also to the cross. "A healthy conviction of sin grows by seeing the patience of God,

---

18. Keller, "Puritan Resources," 22–24. Cf. John Owen, *The Works of John Owen* (Edinburgh: Banner of Truth, 1965), vols. 6–7. See also Sinclair B. Ferguson, *John Owen on the Christian Life* (Edinburgh: Banner of Truth, 1987).

the riches of grace, the suffering of Jesus—all so one would not sin."[19]

The emphasis here is on both conversion and sanctification as a process. It is a process of falling out of love with sin because of a realization of what sin has done to Christ. Thus one finds the motivation for genuine lasting repentance. This sounds strange to modern ears familiar with first praying the sinner's prayer and then working on outward conformity to God's law. Nonetheless, it is eminently biblical in light of Paul's teaching and his own struggle with indwelling sin as recorded in Romans 7. It also places the emphasis on a level of self-understanding that goes deeper than observable behavior.

Keller's six-point outline of Puritan emphases quoted above intersects somewhat with the one we have been using in previous chapters: the sufficiency of Scripture; the definition of biblical counseling; its relationship to psychology and psychiatry; the means and methods of behavioral change; and sin, suffering, and Satan. Keller spends relatively little time on the sufficiency of Scripture. A brief quote from Owen suffices to establish this foundational principle.[20] In terms of the definition of biblical counseling, we have seen how Keller notes that the Puritans would not find themselves fitting in readily to any of the current schools of Christian counseling (including nouthetic). Their approach was to apply the Scriptures on a case-by-case basis to the conscience in ways that varied according to need. This was sometimes cognitively, and sometimes behaviorally, but it always addressed the

---

19. Keller, "Puritan Resources," 25.
20. Keller, "Puritan Resources," 12.

heart. Although they lived before the age of modern psychology, they were students of human nature and recognized the role of temperament as well as physiology in human suffering. Thus, for instance, Packer writes that Baxter's study of man was "genuinely psychological in the modern sense of that word, though carried out in the vocabulary and thought forms of medieval physics and metaphysics."[21] In terms of achieving biblical change, the Puritans gave central place to heart idolatry and the reprogramming of the imagination. They also recognized possible satanic influence. This finds some parallel in the work of Powlison and Welch as has been outlined in the previous chapter.

Although it would be foolish to posit too close a relationship, there is clearly more affinity between the Puritan approach and those of Powlison and Welch than there is between the Puritans and Adams. Thus, not surprisingly, two years after the publication of Keller's article, a very different evaluation of the Puritans appeared from Adams's pen in a *Festschrift* in honor of Westminster's first president, Edmund P. Clowney. Adams contributed a chapter of "Reflections on

---

21. J. I. Packer, "The Redemption and Restoration of Man in the Thought of Richard Baxter: A Study in Puritan Theology" (DPhil thesis, Oxford, 1954), 110. For a helpful discussion of parallels between Baxter and modern psychology, especially cognitive and psychodynamic therapies, as well as his medical model, see Kenneth Roth, "Richard Baxter and the Cure of Souls" (ThM thesis, Reformed Theological Seminary, 1995). To those who object that not all his directions are found in Scripture, Baxter replies in *A Christian Directory*: "Are we not men before we are christians [*sic.*]? And is not the light and law of nature divine? And was the Scripture written to be instead of reason, or of logic, or others subservient sciences? Or must they not all be sanctified and used for divinity?" (p. 5).

the History of Biblical Counseling." His survey begins with the Reformation era. He notes, "Calvin was the first to distinguish sharply counseling (the term he used was *admonition*, a translation of the biblical Greek word *noutheteo*) as a regular, formal obligation of the pastor." From Calvin, Adams moves to the Puritan era, of which he says:

> The Puritan emphasis upon "cases of conscience" was an adaptation of the Reformation concern for counseling. But it was largely deflected from concern for the life of the believer when it frequently degenerated into a discussion of the problems of salvation with which many Puritans busied themselves. A schematic approach emerged in which they attempted to analyze and program conversion in a manner unknown to Scripture (breaking it down into definable steps or stages). Those Puritans who became involved in the preparationist teachings that grew out of this, like many psychologists of the present time, themselves probably unwittingly created most of the "cases of conscience" with which they subsequently dealt. Such Puritans (not all engaged in the activity) were the first Protestant psychologizers of religion, and the effects of their efforts were not unlike those confusing efforts currently seen among evangelicals busy mixing psychological schemes of problem solving with the pure teaching of the Word of God. An in-depth study of this matter in Puritanism might have a salutary effect on the contemporary problem.[22]

---

22. Jay E. Adams, "Reflections on the History of Biblical Counseling," in *Practical Theology and the Ministry of the Church, 1952–1984: Essays in Honor of Edmund P. Clowney*, ed. Harvie Conn (Phillipsburg, N.J.: P&R, 1990), 205.

The charge of preparationism, the idea that sinners should prepare themselves for grace and salvation, is a common criticism.[23] It surfaces also in Keller's article. Nevertheless, Keller observes "these pathologies were not true of all the Puritans to the same degree and do not offset their enormous contributions."[24] (The subject of preparationism would take us beyond the purpose of this study, but for additional comments see the postscript.) It is significant that Adams connects the Puritans' emphasis on understanding processes and motivations of the heart with the modern evangelical psychotherapy movement. His own preference for dealing with observable behavior is apparent and contrasts with the more sympathetic attitude of some of his colleagues like Keller, Powlison, and Welch.

As stated previously, I do not mean to suggest that Welch and Powlison reflect a great deal of direct Puritan influence. However, their emphasis on the heart and their recognition of the implications of being sinned against as well as sinning are compatible with at least indirectly mediated Puritan influences. Their more positive engagement with secular psychology also finds some parallel in Puritan thought, especially that of Baxter.

I would like to suggest that such influences move at least one element of the nouthetic or biblical counseling movement in a direction that offers the kind of biblically corrective

---

23. See Norman Pettit, *The Heart Prepared: Grace and Conversion in Puritan Spiritual Life* (New Haven: Yale University Press, 1966), for the origin of the term.

24. Keller, "Puritan Resources," 40.

critique which Adams claims he enthusiastically welcomes.[25] Perhaps this is the kind of "tuned and adapted form of nouthetic counseling" that Lovelace says "is most likely to help in congregational renewal."[26]

---

25. Adams, *Competent to Counsel*, 269.
26. Lovelace, "Dynamics of Spiritual Life," 218.

Postscript

I stated at the outset that my approach is that of a reporter rather than an expert. It should, however, be apparent that my sympathies lie with the second generation (Powlison and others) and third generation (Lambert and others) of biblical counselors. That said, the greatest degree of helpful cooperation and courtesy I have received, other than from Ron Harris, has been from Donn Arms, executive director of the Institute for Nouthetic Studies. I have had no direct contact with Adams in recent years. He has been in declining health, and Arms can be thought of as his right-hand man and gatekeeper. The criticisms Arms made of my manuscript are his own. But they also reflect things Adams has been saying over the years. The comments that follow are based mainly on a single telephone conversation on February 27, 2014, and my notes of that conversation. We also had significant e-mail correspondence between December 1, 2013, and May 27, 2014.

Arms takes exception to Carter's "condescending" observation that Adams's degrees were in theology and speech, not psychology, and that his training in psychology was limited to a six-week internship with Mowrer, whose influence Adams reflects more than he recognizes. (In fact, as I point out in a footnote, Adams also took a course with a Freudian at Temple University in Philadelphia.) Arms notes that Adams, who majored in Greek at Johns Hopkins University after attending Reformed Episcopal Seminary, is an expert in Greek, and his early interest was in homiletics and preaching more than in counseling.[1] His early interest explains the doctorate in speech. He would not have needed a doctorate from Brigham Young University to criticize Mormonism; neither did he need one in psychology to criticize psychologists. In fact, Adams wears his lack of training in psychology as a badge of honor. The point is that his expertise in Greek and homiletics is much more important to the development of a biblical model of counseling than a training in psychology would have been.

By way of contrast, Arms notes that Adams's critics from the psychology establishment are woefully weak in biblical exegesis and have turf to defend. This is especially true of Carter's exegetically weak and "specious" attempt to argue for the priority of *parakeleō* and its cognates over *noutheteō* and its cognates as an appropriate definition of biblical counseling. Nouthetic counseling, according to Arms, is simply the term used for biblical counseling as defined by Adams. It covers the entire semantic field of appropriate terms.[2]

---

[1]. In a recent (February 1, 2014) interview in *Tabletalk*, Adams states his ministry *foci* as having been exegesis and systematic theology. "A combination of these two disciplines, in particular, kept me from going off base when I began counseling and began to write about it." See Jay Adams, "Competent to Counsel: An Interview with Jay Adams," February 1, 2014, http://www.ligonier.org/learn/articles/competent-counsel-interview-jay-adams/.

[2]. Note, however, the precise definition of nouthetic counseling in chapter 1. At the same time, Adams and Powlison both observe that the precise term used is indifferent, although Powlison also distinguishes between the

A related point is Adams's perceived minimizing of general revelation and common grace. Adams does believe in common grace, but he believes that this concept has been abused by those who, under the slogan "All truth is God's truth," claim that God has revealed truth through unbiblical thought systems. "God does, of course, restrain sin, allow people to discover facts about His creation etc., in common grace...but God never sets up rival systems competitive to the Bible.... This is not common grace."[3] Footnote 8 of chapter 3, which quotes Bookman, is relevant here. It is a common error to understand secular psychology as part of God's general revelation. At best, it is a fallen distortion of that revelation, with "an element of truth" in need of redemption (as Powlison points out in various articles quoted in chapter 3).

There are two other related criticisms of Adams as well. One is that he deals only with external behavior. Another is that he does not take seriously enough that we are not always responsible for our own suffering. Regarding the latter, Arms bristles at my suggestion that, while Adams does affirm that we are not always responsible for our suffering, this does not come across as an emphasis in his writings. The fact is Adams does make this point "robustly," according to Arms. How often does he have to make it before it becomes an emphasis?

---

two in terms of the type of approach needed in specific counseling situations. See Powlison's discussion in chapter 3 under "The Sufficiency of Nouthetic Counseling."

3. Adams, *Theology of Christian Counseling*, 8. Adams also notes that "all error is the devil's error." *A Call to Discernment: Distinguishing Truth from Error in Today's Church* (Eugene, Ore.: Harvest House, 1987), 30.

Regarding the emphasis on the external, both Adams and Arms point out that this is because we cannot read the heart and can only deal with observable behavior. Too much emphasis on internal motives can lead to unhelpful navel-gazing. Here, I believe, we are getting to the crux of the matter. Adams and Arms may well be justified in dismissing their critics from the psychology establishment as being biblically weak. The same cannot be said of those from Adams's own Reformed theological background. Yet, here also, the perception persists that Adams fails to deal adequately with matters of the heart. Think especially of the comments by the Dutch theologians Jonker and Trimp, as well as by Kirwan in chapter 2.

We saw how Adams rejects the "idols of the heart" concept. He and Arms both point out that the Bible deals with idolatry only in terms of physical objects. This is true even of the Ezekiel 14 passage used by proponents of the concept. But see the reference in chapter 1 where Adams (paraphrasing 1 Thessalonians 1:9) states that the Christian life "begins by turning *from* idols/*to* the living and true God." The Thessalonians may have worshiped literal idols, but it seems unlikely that this is what Adams had in mind when applying the concept to the present day.

Jesus in the Sermon on the Mount shows how sins of adultery and murder reach the heart. They go beyond just observable behavior. If this is true of commandments dealing with our duty to our neighbors, surely it also applies to those dealing with our duty to God, including the prohibition of idolatry. I cannot see how it is possible to avoid the force of Powlison's words as both paraphrased and quoted in chapter 3, and repeated here:

The first great commandment to love God with heart, soul, mind, and strength also demonstrates the essential "inwardness" of the law regarding idolatry. "The language of love, trust, fear, hope, seeking, serving—terms describing a relationship to the true God—is continually utilized in the Bible to describe our false loves, false trusts, false fears, false hopes, false pursuits, false masters."

If *idolatry* is the characteristic Old Testament word for "our drift from God," then *desires* is the New Testament equivalent. "The New Testament language of problematic 'desires' is a dramatic expansion of the tenth commandment, which forbids coveting…[and] internalizes the problem of sin, making it 'psychodynamic'".… "[It] lays bare the grasping and demanding nature of the human heart, as Paul powerfully describes it in Romans 7. Interestingly (and unsurprisingly) the New Testament merges the concept of idolatry and the concept of inordinate, life-ruling desires. Idolatry becomes a problem of the heart, a metaphor for human lust, craving, yearning and greedy demand."[4]

Or, to quote Keller:

> We cannot confine idolatry to literal bowing down before the images of false gods. It can be done internally in the soul and heart without being done externally and literally (Ezekiel 14:3ff.). It is substituting some created thing for God in the heart, in the center of life.… In the Bible, then, idolatry is looking to your own wisdom and competence, or to some other created thing, to provide

---

4. See Powlison, "Idols of the Heart," 36.

> the power, approval, comfort and security that only God can provide."[5]

Ezekiel 14, as Adams and Arms point out, is dealing with literal idols; but this does not detract from the fact that it also deals with the heart's attitude to those idols. The same surely applies to exchanging the truth of God for a lie, worshiping and serving the creature rather than the Creator in Romans 1:25. Self-examination is clearly taught in Scripture (2 Cor. 12:5; 1 Peter 1:10–11). Encouraging counselees to engage in it is not the same as claiming to know the state of their hearts.

In chapter 4, with help from Keller in particular, I suggest that the Puritans' emphasis on the heart is a helpful corrective with which some developments in biblical counseling have a certain affinity. Adams rejects this, comparing the Puritans to modern-day psychologists because of their preparationist teachings that "unwittingly created most of the 'cases of conscience' with which they subsequently dealt."[6]

Preparationism, as previously indicated, is the view that the Puritans believed it is necessary for unregenerate people to "prepare" for salvation by using the means of grace such as Bible reading, prayer, church attendance, conviction of sin, and so forth. Sometimes the impression is given that this is possible without the prior work of the Holy Spirit. Packer (an expert on Puritanism, which Adams is not) says this is a misunderstanding of the Puritans. They believed that God alone prepares hearts, instilling a sufficient depth of conviction such

---

5. Keller, *Counterfeit Gods*, 179–80n6.
6. Adams, "Reflections on the History of Biblical Counseling," 205.

that subsequent conversion brings real and lasting character transformation, unlike much modern-day evangelism, which readily accepts verbal professions of faith and (often temporary) surface change.[7] It follows by extension that in the counseling of believers in need of behavioral change, attention to the preparatory convicting work of God's Spirit is the most promising way of ensuring real and lasting change.

The subject of preparationism is part of a larger debate as to whether the Puritan era represented the pinnacle of Reformed orthodoxy or a deviation from it. We obviously cannot engage fully in that debate here. My own view, having grown up in a background heavily influenced by the Puritans, is that the dangers of which Adams warns are not to be disregarded. However, as Keller states, "these pathologies were not true of all the Puritans to the same degree and do not offset their enormous contributions."[8] Perhaps it would be more accurate to say with Packer that the Puritans have been misunderstood. However, as Beeke and Smalley concede in their carefully balanced historical study *Prepared by Grace for Grace: The Puritans on God's Ordinary Way of Leading Sinners to Christ*, some of them at least left themselves open to being misunderstood and misapplied.[9] In any case, Keller,

---

7. J. I. Packer, *A Quest for Godliness: The Puritan Vision of the Christian Life* (Wheaton, Ill.: Crossway, 1990), 298. The term *counseling* is also used for the direction given to professed converts at evangelistic campaigns, but clearly the meaning is different from what we have been discussing.

8. Keller, "Puritan Resources," 44.

9. Joel R. Beeke and Paul M. Smalley, *Prepared by Grace for Grace: The Puritans on God's Ordinary Way of Leading Sinners to Christ* (Grand Rapids: Reformation Heritage Books, 2013), 251–54. This is the best book of which I am aware on the Puritan doctrine of preparation, not *for* grace, but

Powlison, and others who evidence some Puritan influence either directly or indirectly cannot be justly accused of an excessive degree of introspection and navel-gazing. Their goal is to help counselees gain a greater biblical self-understanding in order that, with the empowerment of the Holy Spirit, they can make more than surface changes. This is surely a positive development in biblical counseling.

---

by grace for grace. The authors place this in the context of church history from Augustine to Calvin and distinguish it from the Roman Catholic idea of self-preparation. Sinclair B. Ferguson, in the foreword, makes the valid observation that too much research on the Puritans has been done by academics unrelated to the pastoral concerns with which the Puritans dealt.

Bibliography

Adams, Jay E. *A Call to Discernment: Distinguishing Truth from Error in Today's Church*. Eugene, Ore.: Harvest House, 1987.

———. *The Christian Counselor's Manual: The Practice of Nouthetic Counseling*. Grand Rapids: Zondervan, 1973.

———. *Competent to Counsel*. Phillipsburg, N.J.: Presbyterian and Reformed, 1970. Reprint, Grand Rapids: Zondervan, 1986.

———. "Competent to Counsel: An Interview with Jay Adams." Posted February 1, 2014. Accessed November 25, 2014. http://www.ligonier.org/learn/articles/competent-counsel-interview-jay-adams/.

———. *Essays on Counseling*. Nutley, N.J.: Presbyterian and Reformed. Reprint, Grand Rapids: Zondervan, 1972. Originally *The Big Umbrella and Other Essays on Christian Counseling*.

———. "For Now…" Posted October 1, 2010. Accessed November 25, 2014. www.nouthetic.org/blog/?p=3845.

———. "The Heart of the Matter." Posted May 7, 2012. Accessed November 25, 2014. www.nouthetic.org/blog/?p=792.

———. *How to Help People Change: The Four-Step Biblical Process*. Grand Rapids: Zondervan, 1986.

———. *Marriage, Divorce and Remarriage in the Bible*. Grand Rapids: Zondervan, 1980.

———. *The Power of Error: Demonstrated in an Actual Counseling Case.* Grand Rapids: Baker, 1978.

———. *Ready to Restore: The Layman's Guide to Christian Counseling.* Phillipsburg, N.J.: Presbyterian and Reformed, 1981.

———. "Reflections on the History of Biblical Counseling." In *Practical Theology and the Ministry of the Church, 1852–1984*, edited by Harvie Conn, 203–17. Phillipsburg, N.J.: Presbyterian and Reformed, 1990.

———. "Second Generation Counselors?" Posted June 16, 2010. Accessed November 25, 2014. www.nouthetic.org/blog/?p=3845.

———. *A Theology of Christian Counseling: More Than Redemption.* Grand Rapids: Zondervan, 1979.

———. *What about Nouthetic Counseling?* Grand Rapids: Baker, 1976.

———. *What Do You Do When Anger Gets the Upper Hand?* Nutley, N.J.: Presbyterian and Reformed, 1975.

———. *What Do You Do When Fear Overcomes You?* Nutley, N.J.: Presbyterian and Reformed, 1975.

———. *What Do You Do When You Become Depressed?* Nutley, N.J.: Presbyterian and Reformed, 1975.

———. *What to Do about Worry.* Phillipsburg, N.J.: Presbyterian and Reformed, 1980.

Arms, Donn R. "Institute for Nouthetic Studies: Monthly Archives: September 2013." Posted September 12, 2013. Accessed November 25, 2014. www.nouthetic.org/blog/?p=6206.

———. "Institute for Nouthetic Studies: Monthly Archives: October 2013." Posted October 29, 2013. Accessed November 25, 2014. www.nouthetic.org/blog/?p=6340.

Baxter, Richard. *The Practical Works of Richard Baxter.* Vol. 1, *A Christian Directory.* Ligonier, Pa.: Soli Deo Gloria, 1990.

———. "What Are the Best Preservatives against Melancholy and Overmuch Sorrow?" In *The Morning Exercises at Cripplegate*, vol. 3. Wheaton, Ill.: Richard Owen Roberts, 1981.

Beeke, Joel R., and Paul M. Smalley. *Prepared by Grace for Grace: The Puritans on God's Ordinary Way of Leading Sinners to Christ*. Grand Rapids: Reformation Heritage Books, 2013.

Bettler, John. "Biblical Counseling: The Next Generation." *Journal of Pastoral Practice* 8, no. 4 (1989): 8–11.

———. "Counseling and the Problem of the Past." *Journal of Biblical Counseling* 12, no. 2 (Winter 1994): 5–23.

Brooks, Thomas. *The Works of Thomas Brooks*. Edited by Alexander B. Grosart. 6 vols. Edinburgh: Banner of Truth, 1980.

Carlson, David E. "Jesus' Style of Relating: The Search for a Biblical View of Counseling." *Journal of Psychology and Theology* 4, no. 3 (Summer 1976): 181–92.

Carter, John D. "Adams' Theory of Nouthetic Counseling." *Journal of Psychology and Theology* 3, no. 3 (Summer 1975): 143–55.

Carter, John D., and Bruce Narramore. *The Integration of Psychology and Theology: An Introduction*. Grand Rapids: Zondervan, 1979.

Charnock, Stephen. *Discourses upon the Existence of God*. Grand Rapids: Baker, 1979.

Coe, John H. "Educating the Church for Wisdom's Sake or Why Biblical Counseling Is Unbiblical." Unpublished paper. Evangelical Theological Society, 1991.

Crabb, Larry. *Basic Principles of Biblical Counseling*. Grand Rapids: Zondervan, 1975.

———. *Effective Biblical Counseling: A Model for Helping Caring Christians Become Capable Counselors*. Grand Rapids: Zondervan, 1977.

———. *The Marriage Builder: A Blueprint for Couples & Counselors*. Grand Rapids: Zondervan, 1982.

———. *Understanding People: Deep Longings for Relationship*. Grand Rapids: Zondervan, 1987.

Deckard, Mark. *Helpful Truth in Past Places: The Puritan Practice of Biblical Counseling*. Fearn, Ross-shire: Christian Focus, 2010.

Ferguson, Sinclair B. *John Owen on the Christian Life*. Edinburgh: Banner of Truth, 1987.

Fitzpatrick, Elyse. *Idols of the Heart: Learning to Love God Alone*. Phillipsburg, N.J.: P&R, 2001.

Frame, John. *Cornelius Van Til: An Analysis of His Thought*. Phillipsburg, N.J.: P&R, 1995.

———. *The Doctrine of the Knowledge of God*. Phillipsburg, N.J.: Presbyterian and Reformed, 1987.

Hielema, J. S. *Pastoral or Christian Counseling: A Confrontation with American Pastoral Theology, in Particular Seward Hiltner and Jay E. Adams*. Utrecht: Elinkwijk, 1975.

Holifield, E. Brooks. *A History of Pastoral Care in America: From Salvation to Self-Realization*. Nashville: Abingdon Press, 1983.

Hurding, Roger. *The Tree of Healing*. Grand Rapids: Zondervan, 1985.

Johnson, Eric. *Foundations for Soul Care: A Christian Psychology Proposal*. Downers Grove, Ill.: InterVarsity, 2007.

Johnson, Eric, and Stanton L. Jones, eds. *Psychology & Christianity: Four Views*. Downers Grove, Ill.: InterVarsity, 2000.

Keller, Timothy. *Counterfeit Gods: The Empty Promises of Money, Sex, and Power, and the Only Hope That Matters*. New York: Riverhead Trade Books, 2011.

———. "Puritan Resources for Biblical Counseling." *Journal of Pastoral Practice* (1988): 11–44.

Bibliography

Kirwan, William T. *Biblical Concepts for Christian Counseling: A Case for Integrating Psychology and Theology*. Grand Rapids: Baker, 1984.

Kittel, Gerhard, ed. *Theological Dictionary of the New Testament*. Vol. 4. Translated by G. W. Bromiley. Grand Rapids: Eerdmans, 1967.

Lambert, Heath. *The Biblical Counseling Movement after Adams*. Wheaton, Ill.: Crossway, 2012.

Lloyd-Jones, D. Martyn. *Healing and the Scriptures*. Nashville, Tenn.: Oliver-Nelson Books, 1988.

Lovelace, Richard F. *Dynamics of Spiritual Life: An Evangelical Theology of Renewal*. Downers Grove, Ill.: InterVarsity, 1979.

MacArthur, John. *Our Sufficiency in Christ*. Wheaton, Ill.: Crossway, 1998.

MacArthur, John, and Wayne Mack. *Introduction to Biblical Counseling: A Basic Guide to the Principles and Practice of Counseling*. Dallas: Word Publishing, 1994.

MacDonald, James, Bob Kellemen, and Stephen Viars. *Christ-Centered Biblical Counseling: Changing Lives with God's Changeless Truth*. Eugene, Ore.: Harvest House, 2013.

Mack, Wayne A. *A Homework Manual for Biblical Counseling*. Phillipsburg, N.J.: Presbyterian and Reformed, 1980.

Owen, John. *The Works of John Owen*. Edited by William Goold. 16 vols. Edinburgh: Banner of Truth, 1965.

Packer, J. I. Foreword to *Introduction to Puritan Theology: A Reader*, edited by Edward E. Hindson. Grand Rapids: Baker Academic, 1976.

———. *A Quest for Godliness: The Puritan Vision of the Christian Life*. Wheaton, Ill.: Crossway, 1990.

———. "The Redemption and Restoration of Man in the Thought of Richard Baxter: A Study in Puritan Theology." DPhil thesis, Oxford, 1954.

Pettit, Norman. *The Heart Prepared: Grace and Conversion in Puritan Spiritual Life*. New Haven: Yale University Press, 1966.

Powlison, David. "25 Years of Biblical Counseling: An Interview with Jay Adams and John Bettler." *Journal of Biblical Counseling* 12, no. 1 (Fall 1993): 8–13.

———. "Affirmations and Denials: A Proposed Definition of Biblical Counseling." *The Journal of Biblical Counseling* 9, no. 1 (Fall 2000): 18–25.

———. *The Biblical Counseling Movement: History and Context*. Greensboro, N.C.: New Growth Press, 2010.

———. "Critiquing Modern Integrationists." *Journal of Biblical Counseling* 11, no. 3 (Spring 1993): 24–34.

———. "Crucial Issues in Contemporary Biblical Counseling." *Journal of Pastoral Practice* 9, no. 3 (1988): 53–78.

———. "Cure of Souls & the Modern Psychotherapies." *Westminster Today* 4:1 (Summer 2011): 6–9.

———. "David Powlison Endorses the Name Change: Thoughts and Comments on the Name Change to ACBC from Powlison of CCEF." Posted October 9, 2013. http://www.biblicalcounseling.com/blog/david-powlison-endorses-the-name-change.

———. Foreword to *Christ-Centered Biblical Counseling: Changing Lives with God's Changeless Truth*, by James MacDonald, Bob Kellemen, and Stephen Viars. Eugene, Ore.: Harvest House, 2013.

———. "How Does Scripture Teach Us to *Redeem* Psychology?" *The Journal of Biblical Counseling* 26, no. 3 (Spring 2012): 18–27.

———. "Idols of the Heart and 'Vanity Fair.'" *The Journal of Biblical Counseling* 13, no. 2 (Winter 1995): 35–50.

———. "Integration or Inundation?." In *Power Religion*, edited by Michael Scott Horton, 191–218. Chicago: Moody Press, 1992.

———. "Larry Crabb and Biblical Counseling." In *Theology and Secular Psychology: Resource Articles*, 1–15. Glenside, Pa.: Westminster Campus Bookstore, 1992.

———. *Power Encounters: Reclaiming Spiritual Warfare*. Grand Rapids: Baker, 1995.

———. "Which Presuppostions? Secular Psychology and the Categories of Biblical Thought." *Journal of Psychology and Theology* 12, no. 4 (1984): 270–78.

Roth, Kenneth. "Richard Baxter and the Cure of Souls." ThM thesis, Reformed Theological Seminary, 1995.

Smith, Winton. "The Biblical Counseling Movement after Adams." Posted February 2012. http://www.reformation21.org/shelf-life/the-biblical-counseling-movement-after-adams.php.

Trench, R. C. *Synonyms of the New Testament*. Grand Rapids: Eerdmans, 1948.

Van Til, Cornelius. *Christian Theistic Ethics*. Nutley, N.J.: Presbyterian and Reformed, 1971.

Welch, Edward T. *Blame It on the Brain?* Phillipsburg, N.J.: P&R, 1998.

———. "Codependency and the Cult of Self." In *Power Religion*, edited by Michael Scott Horton, 219–43. Chicago: Moody Press, 1992.

———. *The Counselor's Guide to the Brain and Its Disorders: Knowing the Difference between Disease and Sin*. Grand Rapids: Zondervan, 1991.

———. *Depression: A Stubborn Darkness*. Greensboro, N.C.: New Growth Press, 2004.

———. "Helping Those Who Are Depressed." *Journal of Biblical Counseling* 18, no. 2 (Winter 2000): 25–31.

———. "Is Biblical-Nouthetic Counseling Legalistic? Reexamination of a Biblical Theme." *Journal of Pastoral Practice* 11, no. 1 (1992): 4–21.

———. "Understanding Depression." *Journal of Biblical Counseling* 18, no. 2 (Winter 2000).

———. *When People Are Big and God Is Small: Overcoming Peer Pressure, Codependency, and the Fear of Man*. Phillipsburg, N.J.: P&R, 1997.